# 36
# Short Walks
# Visiting
# Chiltern Pubs

*Christopher Porter Brown*

*Illustrations*
*Philip Allsopp*

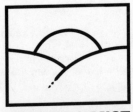

**MORNING MIST
PUBLICATIONS**

First Published 1994
This edition 1996

©Morning Mist Publications

ISBN 1 874476 12 8

**Cover: The Crooked Billet, Stoke Row**

**Designed by Morning Mist Publishing**

Printed and bound in Great Britain by
Biddles Ltd, Guildford and King's Lynn

# The Chilterns

1. Luton
2. Tring
3. Wendover
4. High Wycombe
5. Henley
6. Goring

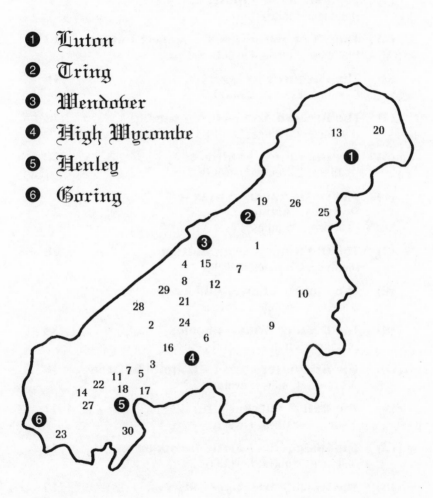

# Index

# $\mathfrak{Index}$ Cont.

# Introduction

The Chiltern hills have long been recognised as a landscape of great beauty. Famous for rolling hills and majestic beech woods the Chilterns are also worth visiting for another treasure, the unique country pub. In this book I have attempted to present a balance of the differing Chiltern landscapes together with a varied selection of pubs which range from the traditional inn to the increasingly popular family style hostelry.

The two primary rules in selecting the walks are:

(a) beautiful scenery

(b) real ale

Every pub featured serves real ale and these are the only beers I have listed at the end of each pub description.

This book is not intended for the walker who wants to clock up the miles. Instead, I recommend you keep to another rule - take your time, enjoy the scenery and above all enjoy the pubs!

## Using This Guide

The walks are listed in order of distance (the shortest first), together with an 'at a glance' guide to the ease of the walk. This guide is shown as a 'Level' and is listed at the start of each walk as well as in the Index. There are three Levels:-

**Level A** - Easy. Short distance, mostly flat with easy route finding.

**Level B -** Moderate. One or two slopes with route finding generally very easy but extra care may be required.

**Level C -** Advanced Slightly longer in distance but easy if you are reasonably fit. One or more steep climbs and some paths may be undefined.

Your confidence in route finding and general level of fitness will determine which walk you choose, though even the longest walk should be easily managed by the averagely fit adult.

A good description of each pub is given and to help, a simple key at the end of each description highlights the main features, such as separate restaurant, children's room, etc. I hope that eventually you will have tried every pub, even if you do not attempt every walk! ~

## Getting There, Parking and Route Finding

Most of the walks start from a parking area and meet the pub en route A few start and finish at the pub, though you can of course, start and finish at every pub should you wish to do so. If you do, please only use the pub car park If you Intend being a patron on the day. When roadside parking is the only option, please remember to be considerate to the local Inhabitants. It is the responsibility of the individual to ensure that the car is parked safely, not obstructing access and most importantly, legally.

Although a sketch map is provided, I recommend you take an Ordnance Survey Landranger Map. The relevant map Is listed at the beginning of each walk. Each starting point in addition to a description on how to get there, is given a grid reference point for quick location on the Landranger Map.

Nearly all the paths followed are marked on the Landranger Map and most are well trodden, so route finding should not be a problem. It is useful to familiarise yourself with the various path signs. The most obvious are the signs which actually say 'footpath' or 'bridleway' (a bridleway is a path open to cyclists and horse riders as well as people on foot), though much more common now are coloured arrows. Yellow denotes footpaths and blue, bridleways. A red arrow is a route open to all traffic. There is also a rapidly growing array of signs which designate specific walks such as long distance paths or nature trails. Where you follow these, I have included a description of the sign

The routes are fairly simple and if you take your time (don't rush even if it is near closing time!), study the map and directions carefully, you should complete your walk without mishap. If you do wander off the trail it is all the more important you are carrying a Landranger map, as it will not only help you find out where you went wrong, but also how you rejoin the walk.

## Clothing

The English are always talking about the weather and for good reason. It is unreliable and unpredictable. For this reason, it is important to be sensibly dressed and prepared for any change. Take a small rucksack or an easy to carry bag and pack a jumper and waterproofs. Nine times out of ten you probably will not need them, but you will be thankful when you do. Many of the paths can be uneven and muddy so comfortable and sturdy footwear is sensible Flip-flops or high heels are definitely not recommended.

## Pub Etiquette for Walkers

The fact that a pub is featured in this book is not a guarantee that you will be welcomed by the landlord, especially if you proceed to tread mud all over the carpet. Generally, walkers are welcome but this will only remain the case if they treat the pub with respect. To preserve a welcome for other walkers, please observe the following simple good manners.

• Only use the pub car park if you intend being a patron of the pub on the day.

• Unless the landlord gives permission, do not eat your own food on the pub premises. Not only is it rude, but you are probably missing out on some good pub grub.

• Do not wear your muddy boots in the bar. Instead leave them outside. The same goes for wet and muddy clothing.

• If you are walking as a group, telephone the pub in advance. This is both polite and practical, especially if you want to be assured of a hot meal.

• Do not assume children or dogs will be welcome. Where available, I have provided this information in the pub description but landlords and rules change. If in doubt, telephone first.

## The Changing Countryside

Every walk and pub has been carefully researched and checked to ensure the walks and pub descriptions are correct. Time however, does not stand still and changes may and probably will occur in the lifetime of this book. A new landlord can rapidly change a pub as can a new farmer the countryside. Although we have made every effort to ensure the details in this book are correct, we accept no liability for errors, omissions or for any consequences arising from the use of this book. Any opinions on the pubs featured are purely those of the author.

## The Country Code

Please ensure you follow The Country Code at all times (see inside front cover).

# The Full Moon
# - Hawridge

*Freehouse. The Full Moon is an old coaching inn and has been licenced for 300 years, having reached its third century in 1993. The building is Grade II listed and rumour has it that at one time it was the local whorehouse! In fact, it is believed that Hawridge Is a deviation of 'whores ridge'! A fine traditional country pub it has lots of wooden beams, a flagstone floor and exposed brickwork giving a truly rustic atmosphere The attractive bar is also made of brick and wooden beams. There are two main spacious seating areas with a cosy seating nook around a splendid fireplace with bench seats and small tables. There is a separate restaurant which can also be used as a function room. A varied bar menu serves everything from sandwiches, rolls and snacks to three-course meals both lunchtimes and evenings, with a dessert menu being featured on a blackboard. Outside is a large lawned garden with tables and wooden bench seats. An inhabited dovecote stands outside the pub in the car park. Well-behaved children are welcome as are dogs on leads! It is requested that muddy boots be left outside.*

     *12.00 noon - 3.00 p m., 6.00 p.m. - 11.00 p.m.*
*Normal Sunday opening*

9

**Beers:**  Courage - Best
Morrells - Best
Ruddles - Best
Ushers - Best
Guest Beer - changed every 2 weeks

## Terrain

Gently undulating through open common and fields. Some of the paths can be thick with undergrowth in summer so wear appropriate clothing.

## Getting to the Start (Grid Ref. 935070)

The walk starts from Cholesbury Common opposite The Full Moon. Getting there is quite complicated so I have given precise instructions. From Tring High Street turn into Akeman Street. At the end of Akeman Street turn right into Park Road and immediately left into Hastoe Lane. Continue straight on for approximately 2½ miles, ignoring two roads off to the right signposted to Hastoe. As you pass the second road off to the right Hastoe Lane becomes Kiln Road. At a three way junction turn right. Continue for a short distance until the road bears left and comes to a junction signposted Hawridge. Turn left and The Full Moon is just ahead on the right opposite Hawridge Common. Alternatively, from Wendover, take the road signposted to Tring. After approximately 1½ miles, after passing through Halton, turn right at the signpost marked Cholesbury. This well signposted road then leads straight through to The Full Moon.

## The Walk

**(1)** To start, with your back to the pub, cross the road and bear diagonally left across the common, passing between a 'No Parking Beyond This Point' sign and stone obelisk on your left. Immediately after this beside a wooden post with a walker on it, fork right and continue ahead, ignoring a smaller path immediately on your right. After a short distance go over a crossing path beside another post with a walker and follow the path ahead to later meet another fork. Take the righthand path going gently downhill and ignore any further turnings off to shortly arrive at a T junction in the form of a very well used path. Turn left along this, ignoring all turnings off and when it eventually bends left, leave it to follow a track ahead to after approximately 20 metres arrive at a lane in front of a house.

¼ mile **(2)** Cross the lane and follow a drive ahead for a few paces before turning left onto a path, virtually maintaining your direction, and passing another house on your right. At the next lane turn left, and after approximately 20 metres, right, onto a signposted public footpath. This follows the lefthand edge of a field, now left to run wild, before coming out at the large earth beech covered ramparts of Cholesbury Hill Fort. Cholesbury Hill Fort is a large Iron Age camp enclosing just over fifteen acres of land and is one of the best preserved examples in the Chilterns. When it was in use, the earth ramparts would have been topped by a wooden stockade. To ward off potential enemies it was common practice to erect the heads of victims of battle on poles around

*10*

the stockade. Turn right and follow the course of the ramparts (it is entirely up to you whether you walk along the top of the bank or the ditch bottom) to eventually pass through a kissing gate onto a track.

**(3)** Turn left along the track to soon arrive at the pretty village church of ½ mile St. Lawrence. The church dates from the 13th century and actually stands within the ramparts of the hill fort. As you arrive at the church leave the gravel path and bear left across the graveyard, passing to the left of the church. Leave the churchyard by a kissing gate and bear right across a small field to shortly go over a stile on your right. Continue along the righthand edge of the next field and at the far side go over another stile, to follow a track ahead to come out at a lane beside Cholesbury village hall.

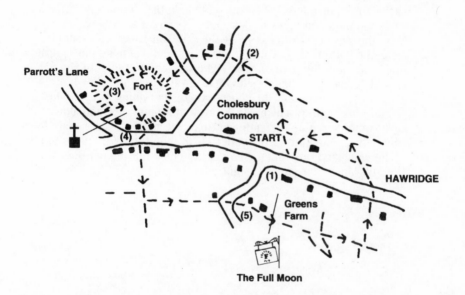

The Full Moon

**(4)** Turn right along the lane and after a few paces left onto a signposted ¾ mile ◆footpath which can be quite hidden. As a guide it is just before you reach Parrotts Lane on your right. After passing between houses, cross a stile into a field and continue ahead along the lefthand edge of the field, descending into a valley. As you descend, to your left you will see the top of the old windmill which marks the site of The Full Moon pub. At the bottom of the valley go over a stile and maintain your route ahead for a few metres before going over a stile on your left. Follow the field edge as though making for the windmill and at the far side go over another stile and continue in the same direction across two more fields before passing to the right of a barn to come out at a lane.

**(5)** Cross the lane and follow a tarmac drive the other side passing to the right of Greens Farmhouse, after which the footpath becomes a track and passes to the right of some kennels. Go over a stile ahead and proceed in the same direction along the righthand edge of a narrow field. At the far side clamber over a fence ahead as best you can and follow a narrow path ahead through scrub. Shortly after entering an area of beech woodland, take a path left leading up the side of a valley. (This path is unmarked and fairly easy to miss and as a guide is a few paces after passing a derelict gate, and almost opposite a path joining from the right.) The path climbs out of the wood and continues between fields to eventually arrive at a road bordering Hawridge Common. Cross the road and join a path the other side traversing the common. Go over two crossing paths descending into another valley, and at the third crossing path before you reach the bottom of the valley, turn left and follow this along the valley side. After a while the path continues to descend through an area of woodland. Near the bottom it almost joins the path on your right, running along the bottom of the valley. Remember, I said almost, make sure you do not join the path on your right but keep to the path you are on which from here bears gently left, away from the valley bottom path, to then maintain its course along the valley side. After a meandering course which involves many minor ups and downs, never quite reaching the valley bottom, the path makes a definite bend left to climb out of the valley. At the top the path bursts free of the woodland onto open common, to come out almost opposite The Full Moon, our starting point.

12

**Ordnance Survey Landranger Map 165**

# The Three Horseshoes
## - Bennett End

*Freehouse. This picturesque 18th century inn is situated in an idyllic position In acres of unspoilt countryside with spectacular views from the garden and through the windows of the lounge bar and dining room. The lounge and dining room are heated by a log burning stove with the added comfort of a carpet, having been refurbished in a relatively modern style. In contrast, the tiny snug public bar remains as it has for centuries with a flagstone floor and a large open fire still with its old oven. A bar snack menu of light meals is available at lunchtimes and a full varied traditional pub menu is served in the evenings, except on Sunday when traditional Sunday lunch is served Instead. If you find it hard to leave this oasis of traditional comfort, the pub offers overnight accommodation.*

 *12.00 noon- 3.00p.m., 7.00p.m.-11.00p.m.*
*Normal Sunday opening, Closed on Mondays.*

**Beers:** Adnams - Bitter
Brakspears - Bitter
Marstons - Pedigree
Guest Beers

## Terrain

Apart from the steep ascent of Bledlow Ridge the going Is fairly easy throughout. After a short stretch of lane walking the way is mostly through fields in an area of outstanding beauty. Take your time and you will thoroughly enjoy this walk.

## Getting to the Start (Grid Ref.783973)

The walk starts from the pub itself which has a fairly large car park, somewhat essential as the narrow lanes hereabout, make it almost impossible for roadside parking. A maze of lanes lead to The Three Horseshoes but perhaps the best way is to take the A40 to West Wycombe, and from there take the road to Bledlow Ridge. After this take the first road left, Bottom Road, and follow it to its end. Turn right and then left onto Town End Road and follow this for approximately ⅓ mile until you reach a small green. Turn right and you will arrive at The Three Horseshoes. Alternatively, you can take Mud Banks Lane from the A40 near Stokenchurch and follow this to the bottom of a valley and beside a pond turn left into Town End Road and follow this to the green mentioned above.

## The Walk

**(1)** To start, facing the pub turn right and follow the lane downhill to the bottom of Bennett End. At the bottom, turn left along another lane and follow this along the bottom of the valley, passing some beautiful traditional Chiltern cottages along the way. After approximately ⅓ mile you will meet a T Junction (Town End Road) in front of a small pond.

½ mile

**(2)** Turn right at the T junction in the direction of the sign for Stokenchurch, West Wycombe and High Wycombe and after approximately 20 metres, turn left on to Bottom Road and follow it walking in the direction of a sign for West Wycombe and High Wycombe. Follow the road until you see a signposted public footpath on your left (a distance of approximately 100 metres). The sign can be easily missed and as a guide it is opposite some relatively modern houses, just before you reach Radnage Pumping Station on your left. Pass through a gate and follow a path to the left of the pumping station and thereafter between fields, now beginning to ascend gently.

¾ mile

**(3)** At the far side of the field turn left, going over a stile and immediately right over another stile. Your route is now along a narrow path climbing the steep side of Bledlow Ridge and passing through an area of woodland where, in summer, the undergrowth can be quite thick. This together with the steep climb can, at times, make the going quite difficult. As you near the top you will meet another stile and you can gain comfort with the knowledge that the hardest part of the walk is now over. Go over the stile and follow a somewhat undefined grass path ahead After a few paces, bear left, to follow the path across a pleasant area of natural grass chalkland which, in summer, is a mass of wild flowers. At this point it is worth making a short detour uphill to your right to gain a lovely view over the valley below. As you reach the far side of the clearing the path becomes more prominent making a gradual descent. On meeting a fence ahead, turn left, to follow the fence and after a short distance go over another stile into a field.

**(4)** Follow the perimeter fence on your left for a few paces and then when you come out to an open field bear diagonally right across it, heading for Radnage Church (not always visible In summer). As you near the perimeter of the field, head for a stile and cross this into another field and maintain your direction heading for a stile visible in the field corner, beside the churchyard wall. Go over the stile and over the churchyard wall to follow a well worn path through the churchyard, keeping a bank on your right After a few paces when this ends, bear gently right, heading for the church porch. The church dates from the 12th century and inside has some medieval wall paintings only recently discovered. 1½ miles

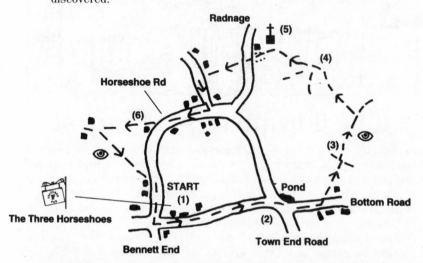

**(5)** From the porch follow a brick path to exit the churchyard and follow a tarmac drive ahead to meet a lane. Cross the lane and go over a stile the other side and continue ahead across the middle of a small field, a mass of buttercups and clover in summer. At the far side of the field go over a stile and turn left along a lane, and after approximately 50 metres turn right into Horseshoe Road. Follow Horseshoe Road uphill and when you see a concrete drive on your right, go over a stile beside it and follow a narrow footpath uphill. 1⅓ miles

**(6)** After going through a gate, turn right along the edge of a field, still going uphill. The views to your left are of the earlier part of the walk. At the top corner of the field turn left, almost going back on yourself, to follow a signposted footpath across the field centre. You now have, probably, the best view on the walk. At the bottom of the field pass through a gap in the hedge and turn right to follow Horseshoe Road once more and it is only a matter of a few paces before you are greeted by the welcome sight of The Three Horseshoes, our starting point. 1¾ miles

2 miles

*15*

### Ordnance Survey Landranger Map 175

# The Chequers – Fingest

*Brakspears. The tiny village of Fingest has only 35 inhabitants. Situated opposite the 12th century Norman church The Chequers' first recorded licensee was a Mrs. Smith in 1720. However, the flintstone and tile hung building can be traced back in part to the 15th century. A splendid feature of the pub is its huge garden which backs onto open countryside. Inside the seating areas are situated around the bar, two of them being sunken and overlooking the garden, both having French windows. Old photos of the nearby village of Turville are on the wall and it is traditionally furnished with ornately carved bench seating and long tables. The original low beamed ceiling and open fires complete a scene which has changed little for centuries. A well-presented cold buffet is available and there is an extensive bar menu featured on a blackboard with two vegetarian choices.*

*1.00 a.m. - 3.00 p.m., 6.00 p.m. - 11.00 p.m.*
*Normal Sunday opening*

**Beers:**  Brakspears - Bitter, OBJ
         Guest Beer

### Terrain
A lovely walk exploring the upper reaches of the Hamble valley. The first half is through fields along the valley bottom with the second half exploring the wooded valley side. The definite highlight Is the incredible view Just before you make your final descent to the pub. Many of the paths can he muddy so come prepared.

### Getting to the Start (Grid Ref.777911)
The walk starts opposite The Chequers pub at Fingest. Fingest can be

reached via the B482 from Stokenchurch. Follow the B482 over the M40 and shortly after you will see Fingest signposted. Alternatively, join the Hamble valley road from the A4155 at Mill End near Henley and follow the road through Skirmett from where Fingest is signposted. Apart from the pub car park, parking is possible in Chequers Lane opposite.

## The Walk

(1) To start, with your back to the pub take the road opposite, Chequers  Lane. Walk past the church and after approximately 50 metres turn right onto a narrow fenced path beside Church Cottage. *The church is famous for its large tower, topped by a double gabled saddleback roof. The graveyard is said to be haunted, possibly by ghosts from the old Bishops palace which once stood beside the church.* The path at first runs between two houses and then comes out at some fields where it forks. Take the righthand fork by continuing along a fenced path between fields, do not go over the stile on your left. Later go over a stile into a field ahead and continue in the same direction along the righthand edge of the field, and at the far side go over another stile to arrive at a track.

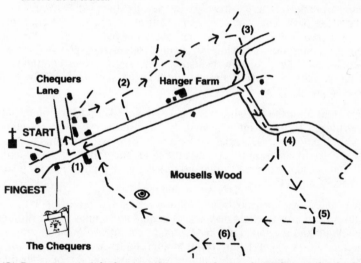

(2) Do not turn right but continue straight on along the track which slowly ¼ mile climbs to meet some outbuildings for the Hanger Estate Forestry Department where the track forks. Take the righthand fork, follow the track until it bends sharp right and at this point leave it to continue ahead along another track which shortly meets a farm gate. Pass through the gate and maintain your route ahead along the track which soon runs along the righthand edge of a field. At the far side leave the track which continues to follow the field edge round, to go over a stile ahead into another field. Maintain your route ahead along the righthand field edge and keep to the field edge as it bends right to soon meet a stile.

1 mile **(3)** Go over the stile and turn right along a lane. A short way along the lane take an unmarked path on your right which almost runs parallel with the lane, and follow this with a hedgerow on your right going gently downhill. To your right now are good views back towards Fingest, identified by its unusual church tower. As you near the bottom of the valley, bear left to meet and follow another lane slgnposted to Frieth, Marlow and High Wycombe. There is a path on the grass verge to the right of the lane to avoid road walking. Follow the lane which gently bends left untll you see a gate on your right and a signposted public bridleway.

1¼ miles **(4)** Leave the lane at this point to follow the bridleway which climbs uphill through woodland, ignoring a path off to your left just after joining. As you climb, ignore any further turnings off, keeping to the main path at all times. Later the path enters an area of lovely, mature, beech woodland and at this point look out for a small oblong pit on your left, which used to be a saw pit. Saw pits were used right up until the beginning of this century. One man would stand in the pit with another on top and together with one saw they would cut logs into planks for easier transportation. Shortly after the saw pit, the bridleway arrives at a crossing path onto which you should turn left, in the direction of a white arrow. A few paces after this follow the path round to the right still in the direction of a white arrow on another tree, ignoring another path ahead. The path now becomes quite narrow and continues to climb until it reaches a prominent crossing path marked by twin wooden posts.

1½ miles **(5)** Turn right onto the crossing path and as before keep to the main path ignoring all turnings off. The path in wet weather can be extremely muddy and it is worth looking out for a number of narrow paths that run parallel to the main route, avoiding the mud. The path eventually bends left and not long after this, after passing between a pair of metal posts, arrives at a track.

1¾ miles **(6)** Turn right along the track which follows a field fence on your left. The track soon leaves the field on your left behind and climbs gently through woodland. Later ignore a marked footpath into Adams Wood on your left and continue to keep to the track to soon after arrive at a field gate. Pass through the gate and maintain your route ahead, going straight across a field, bearing slightly diagonally right. At the far side follow a path into Fingest Wood where you now begin your descent to the Chequers pub at Fingest. At the far side of the wood pass through a gate into an open field and here you are rewarded with one of the best views in the Chilterns. The village in the valley below is Fingest, our finishing point and above on a hilltop is Turville Windmlll which was featured in Chitty Chitty Bang Bang. From our vantage point you can also almost see the entirety of our walk today. Maintain your route downhill,

2½ miles keeping to the lefthand edge of the field, at the bottom go over a stile and follow a track ahead to meet a road. Turn left along the road to arrive back at The Chequers pub, our starting point.

18

# The Bernard Arms - Great Kimble

*The Bernard Arms has strong associations with Chequers, being very close to the Prime Minister's country residence. This is evident in the photographs hanging in the bar of Harold Wilson with his wife Mary taking a farewell drink in the pub before leaving office, and others of Harold MacMillan. In the mid 19th century the pub was actually called The Chequers and was a coaching inn. It is a comfortable, spacious pub with an unusual raspberry pink and green decor and having upholstered bench seating and stools. Food is of a high standard with the seasonal bar menu featured on a blackboard. The restaurant is separate which has a set price menu. The well designed garden has walled, terraced seating areas and a children's swing is in a separate grassed section of the garden.*

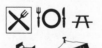

*11.00 a.m. - 3.00 p.m., 6.00 p.m. - 11.00 p.m*
*Normal Sunday openIng*
*Restaurant open Tues - Friday- Lunch and dinner*
*Saturday night and Sunday lunch*

**Beers:**   Benskins - Best Bitter
        Tetley- Bitter
        Wadsworth - 6X
        one Guest Beer

## Terrain

Mostly through level fields and over fine open hillside with some dramatic views. There is one quite long stretch along the B4010 and A4010 which can at times be busy, but this does not detract from the beauty of the walk.

## Getting to the Start (Grid Ref.826065)

The walk starts from a layby at the Junction of the B4010 with the A4010 at Little Kimble, although as it is not far from the layby to the Pub on the A4010, you maywish to start there.

## The Walk

(1) To start, cross the A4010 and turn left the other side to follow the road until you arrive at the Bernard Arms. After the pub, turn right down Church Lane and just after passing the School House join a signposted public footpath on your left. Follow this through a field, passing to the right of a farmhouse and shortly after to the left of a pond, then go over a stile into a second field and turn left along the field edge, to exit via a kissing gate at the field corner.

½ mile

(2) Cross a main road, the A4010, and follow a track uphill the other side signposted as a public bridleway. Continue until you see a kissing gate on your left and here leave the track to pass through the kissing gate and thereafter turn diagonally right along a narrow path going uphill through open grassland. Higher up the path passes to the left of a knoll known as Chequrs Knapp (where fine views can be gained) and shortly after the Knapp you will meet another path which is in fact the Ridgeway long distance path, onto which you should turn left.

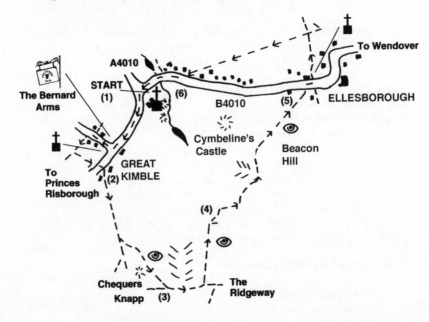

**(3)** Follow the path, guided by the white acorns of the Ridgeway, across a   1¼ miles
grass terrain scarred by banks and ditches created centuries ago by our
ancestors. Later, ignore a signposted footpath off to the left and
continue a little further on to then leave the Ridgeway by going over a
stile on your left. Follow a narrow path ahead with a steep sided valley
to your left to, a short time on, climb over a small rise from where you
will gain some magnificent views. From the top follow a path right that
leads down to a stile. Cross the stile and fork left to after approximately
100 metres, come out at a track.

**(4)** Turn left along the track and go over a tarmac drive to follow a track   1½ miles
the other side. The drive incidentally leads to Chequers, the Prime
Minister's country residence and for a short time we will be walking
through the parkland of the house. Make sure you do not wander from
the route or you could be in for some heavy questioning! As the track
enters a field bear left, then fork right across the centre of the field
heading for a footpath sign visible the other side. At the far side of the
field follow the footpath down some steps skirting the side of a steep
combe, rich in vegetation, the sort of place where my mother used to
tell me Trolls lived. After going over a stile the path comes out onto
open hillside where you must keep to the well worn path across the
hillside, affording more good views as you go. Later as the path skirts
the hill the church tower at Ellesborough will come into view ahead with
the monument at the top of Coombe Hill to your right. From here on,
follow the path down to a stile and go over the stile to thereafter cross
a field heading for Ellesborough Church.

**(5)** Pass through a gate at the field corner and turn right along a road for   2 miles
a few paces to cross the road by a bus stop. Turn right the other side to
follow a tarmac path into the churchyard. The church dates from the
15th century and being close to Chequers has welcomed several Prime
Ministers and world statesmen. The church apart from its beauty is also
renowned for its ghost, a former rector. Once in the churchyard unless
you want to visit the church, bear left to follow a narrow grass path
along the churchyard wall. After passing to the left of the church,
descend some steps through the graveyard to cross a stile the other
side into a field. Walk straight across the field and at the far side go
over another stile and turn left along the edge of a second field. At the
field corner go over a stile and maintain your route across the centre of
another field. Half way across, maintain your direction now with
gardens bordering your path on the left. Shortly after leave the field at
the corner following an enclosed path behind more gardens before
finally bending left to actually pass through a garden and arrive at a
road, the B4010.

**(6)** Turn right along the road and when you see Little Kimble Lodge on your   2½ miles
left, cross the road and follow the pavement the other side. After
passing Little Kimble's 13th century church you will arrive back at the
layby, our starting point.

2¾ miles

# The Old Crown
# - Skirmett

*Brakspear. This pub consists of three cottages converted into one building,
the dining room having once been the village shop. There is a small
courtyard at the front entrance with seating should you wish to be outside,
The cottages date from the 17th century and the building has been a
Brakspear's pub for the past 200 years. Today, it is primarily a restaurant
with a very small bar. displaying a traditional country cottage atmosphere.
The main dining room leads off the bar area, with another small cosy room
to the right of the bar. In this room is an inglenook fireplace straight from
the pages of Grimm's Fairy Tales, with pots and a cauldron hanging from
inside. In one corner is a Singer Treadle sewing machine. The walls of the
pub are adorned with old photographs of the landlady's family. The bar
room which has pine furniture and doors, also features a lovely fireplace,
lit in the winter months, and having copper kettles hanging from the
mantle. Lots of interesting bric a brac decorate this room, such as old
bottles, china plates and horse brasses. A full and varied menu is served
consisting of starters, main courses and desserts, together with such
items as Ploughman's Lunch. Food may be eaten in any of the three rooms.
No children under 10 years of age are admitted.*

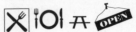   *1.30 a.m. - 2.30 p.m., 6.00 p.m, -11.00 p.m.*
*Normal Sunday opening*

**Beers:** Brakspears - Pale Ale, Special Bitter

**Terrain**
Undulating through fields and along woodland paths with the occasional fine view. The nearest pub is at the beginning where you have a long climb out of the Hamble valley.

**Getting to the Start (Grid Ref.776899)**
The walk starts opposite the pub where there is limited roadside parking. The best way of getting there is via the A4155 and at Mill End near Henley take the road north signposted to Hambleden and Fingest. After approximate 3½ miles you will arrive at Skirmett and The Old Crown.

**The Walk**

(1) Facing The Old Crown, turn right along the road and as the road bends right, turn left onto another road signposted to Frieth and Lane End.  Ignore a signposted footpath on your right and follow the road out of the village, the last building being that of Stud Farm on your left. Just after this, ignore a signposted footpath on your left and a few paces on, take a signposted public bridleway on your right beside a road sign for Skirmett. The bridleway which is somewhat sunken, indicating it is an old route, leads gently uphill and as you climb there are some good views in both directions.

(2) Much further on the path forks, this is marked by a white arrow on a beech tree. Take the lefthand fork and go over an unusual stile built into a disused gate and thereafter follow a path which runs parallel with a fence on your left. The path continues for some distance, winding through woodland before eventually arriving at a stile.          ¾ mile

(3) Go over the stile and ignore the path which continues through the wood on your right, to enter a wide open field. Go straight across the field heading for a cottage directly in front of you. At the far side go over a stile and cross a lane to follow a narrow path the other side which passes to the right of the cottage mentioned. After going over another stile the path continues between fields with some lovely views left over the Hamble valley. The path eventually arrives at a stile on your right beside a bench. Go over the stile and shortly after follow a path along the edge of a garden and thereafter the drive to a cottage, before arriving at a lane.          1¼ miles

(4) Turn left along the lane and after a short distance when this bends sharp right, leave it to continue ahead along a track, marked as both a public bridleway and a public footpath. The track services a number of houses before once again hitting open country with some more fine views to your left over the Hamble valley. As you continue, look out for a narrow path on the left, marked by a white arrow on a post. Take this to start your descent into the valley. Shortly after entering woodland (Adams Wood) you will meet another path onto which you should turn left. Almost immediately after this the path forks. Take the righthand fork which is a footpath and not a bridleway and therefore less muddy.          1¾ miles

23

The path gradually bends left, descending gently to eventually rejoin the bridleway, onto which you should turn right. The descent now becomes steeper and it is not long before the bridleway reaches the edge of the wood. Here you should ignore a path off to your right and maintain your route downhill, the bridleway now running between fields with Skirmett in view directly ahead.

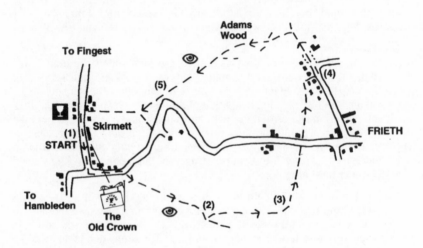

2½ miles **(5)** Just before the bridleway reaches a lane turn right onto a narrow path. Go over a stile and cross a field and at the far side go over another stile, maintaining your route ahead along the righthand edge of another field, heading for the houses of Skirmett the other side. At the far side go over a stile beside a bungalow, and turn right along a track to come out at a lane beside Skirmett village hall. Turn left along the lane passing first the old forge, then another pub in the village. The Frog at Skirmett, a freehouse. Thereafter keep to the lane to arrive back at The Old Crown, our starting point.

2⅓ miles

24

# The Le De Spencer Arms
## - Downley Common

*Fullers. Tucked away off the beaten track the Le De Spencer Arms dates from the 18th century and was originally a bakery as well as a pub. There are rumours of a resident ghost of someone who used to reside at the pub and it is said that 'things happen' but what exactly is not specifically known! It is a charming pub with wood panelled walls and floral wallcovering and curtains. There is a large brick fireplace and wooden beams in the bar which is on two levels. A small room to the side of the bar has two tables. The country style furniture consists of pew seats, wheel back carver chairs and stools. Pictures of rural scenes and studies of cherubic children, together with bric-a-braque and plates emphasise the country rustic character. Food is available and is varied and all home made. A pretty, well maintained garden enhances the exterior which is lawned and has a play area for children. Dogs are also welcome.*

      *11.00 a.m. - 2.30 p.m*
                       *5.30p.m. -11.00p.m. Monday to Friday*
                       *All day Saturday, Normal Sunday opening*

**Beers:** Fullers - ESB, Chiswick, London Pride

### Terrain

Attractive woodland paths and through fields for grazing. The scenery is delightful and for added interest the route passes the National Trust run Hughenden Manor. In places some of the paths can get a little muddy.

25

**Getting to the Start (Grid Ref.864955)**

The walk starts at the car park for the Church of St. Michael & All Angels Hughenden. The church which is beside Hughenden Manor, is off the A4128 just north of High Wycombe.

**The Walk**

(1) The churchyard is the resting place of Beniamin D'Israeli one of our countrys most revered Prime Mlnlsters. There is also a memorial in the chancel to D'Israeli from Queen Victoria. This is unique and is the only example of a memorial erected to a subject by a reigning monarch. Hughenden Manor, passed shortly after, was the home of D'Israeli and it is worth breaking for an hour or so when the house is open for a visit. From the car park, enter the churchyard and follow the wide tarmac path uphill passing to the left of the church to exit the churchyard at the far side beside the beautifully restored Church House. Continue uphill through beautiful open parkland and after passing through a gate turn left along a tarmac drive in the direction of a sign for Deliveries and Disabled Visitors. Unless you want to buy souvenirs or refreshments, ignore the sign for the shop and continue to follow the drive ahead. As it bends left to service Hughenden Manor leave it and continue ahead along a signposted public bridleway which leads quite steeply downhill through woodland. Keep to the bridleway, ignoring all turnings off until you arrive at the far side of the wood and at the bottom of a valley.

½ mile (2) Ignore a path on your left and continue ahead along a fenced path between fields. The path later enters Common Wood where you must ignore two more paths one on either side, to again maintain your route ahead. The path climbs gently to eventually arrive at a junction of paths and tracks beside a National Trust sign for the Hughenden Estate Manor Farm. As before you must ignore all turnings off to maintain your route ahead. Do not make the mistake of forking right immediately after the sign or taklng the path which leads uphill to the left. Instead, ensure you follow a path ahead between these. The path continues to climb to later pass the beautifully simple Well Cottage before meeting a crossing path just before a lane.

1¼ miles (3) Turn right onto the crossing path to go up a short ridge before meeting a track. Turn right along the track and after a few paces when this ends, continue ahead between some wooden posts onto Downley Common. Go gently right across the common heading for some houses at the far side and on meeting a track in front of these, turn left to follow it. Ignore a tarmac lane on your left and maintain your route ahead, still following the track, with houses on your right, to soon arrive at the Le De Spencer Arms.

1½ miles (4) After the pub, continue on the same direction along the track to shortly pass the last of the houses and continue to pass between some wooden posts onto a wooded part of Downley Common. After a short distance look out for and take a marked path (white arrow) which forks right. A few paces on the path passes to the right of a couple of pits and shortly after this meets and goes over a crossing path. This part of the common is riddled with paths and to help you choose the right one, the path you should be following runs along the edge of the wood and you should be able to just make out at first gardens and then fields through the trees on your right. If you keep as near as you can to the edge of the wood with the fields on your right you cannot go wrong.

**(5)** Eventually, if you keep to the path at the edge of the wood you will arrive at a narrow tarmac lane onto which you should turn right. Follow the lane until you see a signposted public footpath on your right and join this by first going over a stile. Thereafter follow a narrow path between fields and after going over a stile, maintain your direction now walking along the righthand edge of a field. Approximately three quarters of the way across the field ignore a stile on your right. Instead, continue to the far corner to go over another stile and thereafter maintain your route ahead along the righthand edge of the next field. Ignore another stile on your right to the wood and just after this as the wood begins to bend right, leave the field edge and maintain your direction by walking across the centre of the field. At the far side go over a stile and turn right along a fenced crossing path. Follow this to shortly arrive at the edge of Hughenden Estate woodland and after passing through a kissing gate turn sharp left to go over a stile into a field.    1¾ miles

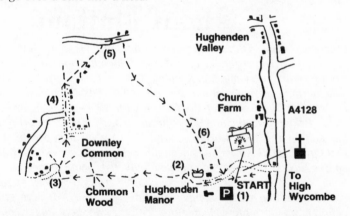

**(6)** Walk along the righthand edge of the field (the narrow end) and at the field corner pass through a gate. Thereafter follow a path downhill through woodland and shortly after ignore a crossing path, maintaining your route downhill along, at times, a particularly narrow path to eventually come out at a concrete path beside a cottage on your left. Follow the concrete path to arrive at the tarmac drive to Hughenden Manor with All Angels Church below you. Turn right along the drive and after a few paces pass through a gate on your left and retrace your steps down through the park to the church car park, our starting point.    2½ miles

2¾ miles

27

# The Old Swan
# - Swan Bottom

*Freehouse. This 16th century coaching Inn's claim to fame is that it appeared as the setting for one of Noel Edmonds' Gotcha Oscars! Its olde worlde style is very much in keeping with its age. A large fireplace with a woodburning stove lies at one end of the bar and.a smaller fireplace in the centre. The flagstone floor fits in well with the exposed beams and brick walls. Bric-a-brac such as brass horns, plates, a copper kettle and stone jug add to the olde worlde charm. As well as a separate a la carte restaurant, a full bar menu is available comprising snacks as well as three course meals. The menu is changed daily, fish being a speciality, all food being freshly prepared and the landlord's grow their own vegetables to complement the varied menus. The inn is set in a 2 acre garden and children and dogs are welcome provided they are kept under control.*

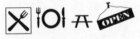

*12.00noon - 3.00p.m., 6.00p.m. - 11.00p.m.*
*Monday to Friday*
*All day Saturday, Normal Sunday opening*

**Beers:**   Bass - IPA
          Fullers - London Pride
          Morland - Bitter
          The above is a typical selection - changed regularly

**Terrain**

An easy walk with no steep gradients mainly along woodland paths and through fields. Peace and quiet guaranteed except at the pub!

## Getting to the Start (Grid Ref.902055)

The walk actually starts from the pub where apart from the pub car park there is limited roadside parking. The easiest way to get there is (a) from Little London on the A413 south of Wendover, take the road to The Lee and Chartridge. At Lee Gate The Old Swan is signposted and as a further guide, is on the lane signposted to St. Leonards; (b) alternatively, from Chesham take the road to Chartridge and continue through the village to Swan Bottom and there take the turning right to St. Leonards. The Old Swan is on the left.

## The Walk

(1) To start, facing the pub, take the track on the left passing between the  pub and some houses on your left. Follow the track to later pass a pretty cottage on your right, just after which the track bends left to enter Lordling Wood. Leave the track at this point and turn right onto another track which runs through the centre of the wood, signposted as a public footpath. Immediately upon joining this ignore two more signposted footpaths on your right. The track is well used and easy to follow through the wood and to reassure you you will see white painted arrows at regular intervals on the trees.

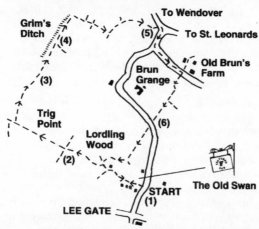

(2) Later, go over a crossing track and maintain your direction now with a field on your right. The track soon narrows and shortly after this forks, where you should keep left still following the white arrows. Some time on the path passes a trig point which standing at a point 232 metres above sea level, is the highest point on the walk. Not long after this you will arrive at a narrow crossing path marked by a white arrow on a tree to the left of the path. Make sure you do not miss this. Turn right here and follow a narrow path through the wood, again being guided by the white arrows. After a short distance you will meet a path joining from the right. Turn left onto this and after about 10 paces turn right, thereby maintaining your original direction and still following the white arrows. Later the path passes between a couple of brick pillars, once an old gateway.

29

1 mile **(3)** Immediately after passing between the brick pillars you will come out at an open area and ahead of you two fields. Bear left here and just before actually entering the field on left, bear right to follow a narrow path through a strip of woodland separating the two fields. The fields soon end and the path continues ahead through another wood, Baldwins Wood. You will now notice a ditch on your right which is an ancient earthwork dating from the Iron Age, known as Grim's Ditch. The reason for such ditches many of which stretch for hundreds of miles, is unclear though the most probable explanation is that they acted as boundaries.

1¼ miles **(4)** On coming out into a field, maintain your direction along the righthand edge. As you approach the far side you may hear a few strange noises to your left from a bird sanctuary. At the far side of the field follow a track ahead which soon bends right. Several metres on where the track bends left leave it to follow an ill-defined track ahead. Make sure you do not miss this. Go over a crossing track to now follow a much easier track through the centre of the wood, once again being guided by the white arrows. At another crossing track turn left and follow this through a large plantation. A short time later ignore a track on your left, continuing to follow the track ahead which shortly after begins to bend gently right. From here on, the track meanders through the wood going gently downhill. You should ignore all turnings off to eventually come out at the far side of the wood where you should follow the track along the righthand edge of a field to a road.

1¾ miles **(5)** Turn right along the road and then right again onto a second road in the direction of the sign for The Lee and Great Missenden. At the top of a small rise turn left onto Arrewig Lane and follow this until you almost draw level with Old Brun's Farm, where you should pass through a hole in the hedge on your right, opposite the signposted footpath on your left. Thereafter continue ahead along the lefthand edge of a field and approximately two thirds of the way across pass through a gap in the hedge on your left. Thereafter maintain your direction along the righthand edge of another field. On reaching the corner of the field go over a stile ahead and maintain your direction along the lefthand edge of the next field. The large white house to your right at the side of the field is Brun's Grange. At the far side of the field go over another stile and continue in the same fashion across the next field to go over a stile at the field corner and meet a lane.

2½ miles **(6)** Cross the lane and follow a signposted footpath across the centre of the field opposite. At the far side follow the path ahead through Lordling Wood, ignoring any turnings off. The path meanders along the edge of the wood and later passes behind the cottage we met at the beginning of the walk, before arriving at a track onto which you should turn left.

2¾ miles After a few paces on meeting a second track, turn left again and follow this thereby retracing your steps at the beginning of the walk, back to The Old Swan, our starting point.

# The Plough
# - Lower Gadsden

*Freehouse. The Plough is the only pub on the Ridgeway long distance walking route and therefore you should find yourself in good company. It is surrounded by trees and has a large garden with bench seats and tables with seating also available on the green in front of the pub. It is very much a traditional style pub with bench seating and stools. A woodburner is at one end of the lounge and an open fireplace at the other. There are two rooms and food may be eaten in either, there being a blackboard menu offering bar snacks and main courses and also a menu featuring Balti food (Indian cuisine). Both rooms are carpeted and there is a collection of bottles and jugs. In one of the rooms is an interesting reed organ*

       *12.00 noon - 2.30 p.m., 5.30 p.m. - 11.00 p.m.*
*Normal Sunday opening*

**Beers:** Benskins - Best
Greene King - Abbots, IPA, Rayments
Wadsworth - 6X
Guest Beer

## Terrain

Hilly following mainly woodland paths. Although the mud and some steep climbs can make this quite a strenuous walk, you are more than rewarded by some beautiful woodland scenery and at times glorious views.

## Getting to the Start (Grid Ref.823036)

The walk starts from the Buckinghamshire County Council Whiteleaf

Hill Car Park and picnic area. The car park lies on the road to Green Hailey and Great Hampden from the A4010 at Monks Risborough. The car park is clearly signposted from the road and is situated just at the top of the Chiltern Ridge.

**The Walk**

**(1)** From the car park, take a well maintained path passing to the right of a Chilterns Woodlands Information sign. Follow the path to shortly join a much wider path, the Ridgeway, also marked by a black post with a blue arrow and white acorn. The white acorn identifies the Ridgeway path. Turn right along the Ridgeway and after approximately 75 metres leave the Ridgeway, turning right onto a signposted public bridleway. Pass through a gap in some fencing (there could be a stile here in future) and thereafter continue along the edge of a typically regal Chiltern beech wood, with fields on your right.

½ mile    **(2)** After approximately ⅓ of a mile the path forks and at this point you should continue straight on, joining the lefthand path, the least prominent of the two, with the righthand path (the bridleway) going uphill. The path you are now following slowly bends left and starts a gradual descent through more lovely beech wood with some good views through the trees on your left over the Vale of Aylesbury. Later the path bends right to meet a much wider path (a bridleway) onto which you should turn left. The bridleway descends quite steeply (ignore a crossing path) and soon after forks. Take the righthand fork and a few paces on in front of a stile, turn left, thereby remaining on the bridleway which is marked by a blue arrow with a white surround. Keep to the bridleway which can, at certain times of the year, be very muddy (beware), ignoring any turnings off to eventually arrive at a road.

**(3)** Cross the road and join a track the other side, still marked as a bridleway. Follow the track behind a small parking area and at the other side ignore a footpath leading uphill on your right to continue straight on, passing a small information board on your right. The track takes you round the side of Pulpit Hill which rises steeply on your right. Later you will meet two paths leading off the main track, one on either side. You should ignore both of these and continue ahead to shortly after arrive at a gate on your left. *1¼ miles*

**(4)** Pass through this to come out onto some lovely natural chalk downland, in summer covered in flowers. Afer passing through the gate turn right and after a few paces turn left to follow a narrow grass path across a low spur with some glorious views of the surrounding countryside. The path gradually descends the side of the spur, making for a golf course in view directly ahead. Behind you rises the hilltop of Pulpit Hill where at its summit is an Iron Age hill fort. As you near the bottom, the natural chalk grassland is criss-crossed by a maze of paths. This can at first appear confusing but if you simply maintain your direction heading for the golf course you will find that you naturally arrive at a wooden kissing gate. Pass through this and follow a path ahead to shortly arrive at a road. Cross the road, turn left and after a few paces, fork right onto Cadsden Road to soon after arrive at The Plough. *1½ miles*

**(5)** To continue, facing the pub. take the bridleway to the left, signposted as the Ridgeway. Follow this uphill a few paces, then fork left in the direction of a yellow arrow and white acorn. Go over a stile and a few paces on fork right to start your ascent of Whiteleaf Hill. At a crossing path continue straight on, now following a track, again in the direction of the Ridgeway signpost. The path becomes steeper as you go and as it eventually begins to level out and at small clearing with a stone post, it is worth not only pausing to catch your breath but also to enjoy a romantic view of a dense beech wood valley. After this, the climb is negligible and it is an easy short walk to the summit of Whiteleaf Hill introduced by a Buckinghamshire County Council sign. *1¾ miles*

**(6)** From the grass summit of the hill there are some stunning views over the Vale of Aylesbury, with Princes Risborough immediately below you. If you walk to a low wooden rail at the edge of the hill you will see immediately before you a chalk cross, cut into the hillside. *The cross known as the Whiteleaf Cross, along wlth its close neighbour the Bledlow Cross, are the only two turf cut crosses in Britain. Its origin is unclear though the most popular theory is that it was converted from an ancient fertility symbol. From our position it is hard to appreciate the impact of t,he cross which is best viewed from a distance.* To continue, facing the view, turn left and follow the Ridgeway along the ridge of the hill. It is now only a matter of a short walk along the Ridgeway to reach the Whiteleaf Hill car park, our starting point. *1½ miles*

*2¾ miles*

# The Bedford Arms
# - Chenies

*As might be guessed from its name this hotel has strong associations with earlier Dukes of Bedford and has always been an inn. Its pretty facade has three bay windows overlooking a small patio. Being an inn it offers accommodation in ten exclusively designed bedrooms. It has an elegant oak panelled restaurant overlooking the garden and serving an extensive a la carte menu. The bar is far less formal and serves an excellent inexpensive bar menu, with desserts listed on a blackboard should you arrive too late for lunch, then cream teas are served from 3.30 p.m. every day. Here can be seen Elizabethan Style stone arched doorways and arched wooden doors. A carved grey stone fireplace has toby jugs at each end of its mantle. Look for the interesting carved figurines which appear to be holding up the back of the bar. A pair of guns are also displayed behind the bar, not to threaten troublemakers with I hope! The bar is furnished with floral carpet and curtains with comfortable wooden and cushioned seats. Outside is a large lawned garden with seating available in the upper area as well as on the patio. Children are welcome.*

*11.30a.m.- 3.00p.m.*
*5.30p.m. -11.00p.m.*
*Normal Sunday opening*

**Beers:**   Marston - Pedigree
            Theakston - XB
            Younger - IPA

**Terrain**

A lovely walk with the first half along woodland paths and the second half through fields following the banks of the enchanting River Chess. There is never a dull moment on this walk and the only problem you are likely to encounter is mud.

**Getting to the Start (Grid Ref.016984)**

The walk starts from Chenies village centre where limited street parking is possible around two small triangular greens. The village is best reached from the A404 just outside Chorleywood. The turning for the village is well signposted.

**The Walk**

(1) To start, standing in the tiny lane which divides the two triangular greens, with the village pump on your left, cross the road ahead and follow a drive the other side marked Private Access to Church, Manor and Rectory only. Follow the drive up to the entrance of Chenies Manor House and in front of the gates turn right and follow a walled path that runs between the Manor House and church. The Manor House which can be visited in summer is of Tudor origin. Through much of its life it was the seat uf the powerful Russell family, Earls and Dukes of Bedford. During the 18th century the family were respected and famous for greatly improving and tastefully modernising the villages they controlled. Chenies is a perfect example, the village has the appearance of having stood on its current site for centuries when In fact it was almost entirely rebuilt during the last century. The church has a chapel containing some magnificent memorials to the Russell family. When the walls end, continue to follow the path downhill and on entering some woodland take the first path on your left now walking along the side of a wooded valley. Stay on the path, ignoring any turnings off, to eventually arrive at a stile at the far side of the wood. Go over the stile and continue ahead along a wide path with fine views to your right over the Chess valley. Later you will spot the magnificent red brick Latimer House at the far side of the valley.

(2) After passing through another stretch of woodland. the path    ½ mile
eventually comes out at a lane. Turn right along the lane and after approximately 20 metres, left onto a signposted public bridleway. Immediately after this bear left again, ignoring a wide track on your right, to follow a much narrower path along the valley side. After nearly ½ mile the path approaches the far side of the wood where you will see a stile ahead. You must turn right approximately 20 metres before you reach the stile, passing through some wooden posts on your right and thereafter follow a wide path down the valley side. Ignore all turnings off and follow the path down to a stile and cross this into a field. Thereafter continue your descent along the righthand

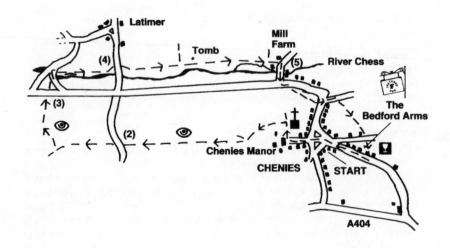

edge of the field with the magnificent Latimer House in view ahead.

**1 mile** **(3)** At the far side of the field, pass through a kissing gate, cross a road and pass through a gate the other side into a small field. Continue straight on across the field and pass through another gate to follow a tarmac drive ahead over the beautiful River Chess. This is probably the most spectacular part of the walk. To your left is a small weir over which excess water tumbles down in a white froth. To your right the river makes its slow way down the valley and immediately before you is the best view you will get of the imposing Latimer House. I think you will agree all this is worth more than just a few seconds pause. Immediately after the river, go over a stile on your right and follow a path through a field and along the river bank. As you approach the far side of the field, bear left away from the river, heading for a stile.

**1¼ miles** **(4)** Go over the stile and cross a lane and another stile into a field. Continue straight on heading for a tree stump with a young oak growing from its centre. Pass to the left of this and thereafter continue straight on across the centre of the field (as a guide the path later meets and follows a line of electricity poles) with good views to your right over the River Chess. Later the path meets and follows the lefthand edge of the field and soon after draws level with a fenced thicket on your right marked Private. Amidst this and barely visible is the ruin of Flaunden Church but I stress this is not accessible. At the far side of the field go over a stile and maintain your direction along the lefthand edge of the next field. Shortly after you will pass a brick tomb to Mr. William Liberty who was buried here in 1777, beside him lies his wife who was buried here thirty five years later - loyalty indeed. The tomb of William Liberty who was a relative of the Liberty's of Regent Street fame, was originally in the grounds of their 18th century mansion house which has long since disappeared. Continue to the far side of the field where you must pass through a gate ahead and thereafter follow a well walked path the other side heading for Mill Farm in front of you, with an arm of the River Chess accompanying you on your right (the farm sells ice cream in summer).

**(5)** After passing through the farmyard turn right along a lane and follow it over two arms of the River Chess, the second bridge crossing beside an old mill. Just after this fork left to arrive at a T junction. Cross the road and turn left the other side and follow it for a short distance until you see some steps on your right opposite Chenies Place. Go up these and thereafter follow a path uphill. On meeting the road again, cross it and join a narrow lane the other side marked unsuitable for motors. Follow this for a short distance until you come to a signposted footpath on either slde. Take the path on the right and follow it uphill along the righthand edge of a field. Approximately two thirds of the way across follow the path behind a fir hedge to soon after come out at a lane. Cross the lane and follow a path through the centre of a field the other side, heading for some houses. After passing between gardens the path comes out at a road beside The Red Lion pub. Cross the road, and turn right the other side to shortly arrive at our featured pub. The Bedford Arms after the pub maintain your direction along the road, taking care of the traffic as from here there is no pavement, to soon arrive back at the village green, our starting point.

2¼ miles

3 miles

# The Bricklayers Arms
# - Hogpits Bottom

*Freehouse. This pretty, ivyclad, listed building has housed a pub for 200 years but probably dates back to the 17th century. It has very much a cosy olde worlde interior with exposed brickwork, wooden beams and lots of bric-a-brac. Pictures of country scenes and guns on thc wall add to the olde worlde atmosphere. The bar and restaurant are carpeted and have traditional cottage style furniture with wooden seats and upholstered stools. The bar area is long and spacious with a raised seating area to one side, guarded by two sculptured bronze dogs. This area has half wood panelled walls and a window at the rear overlooking a field and trees. The bar is decorated with horse brasses and a glass yard measure. Outside is a small paved patio area and a lawned garden. There are also garden benches along the frontage of the pub. A substantial bar menu is on offer and the restaurant provides a la carte service. Daily specials are available from the blackboard in the bar. Food is of a very good standard and may be eaten anywhere inside or out. Chidren are welcome in the dining area and dogs too are welcome as long as they are kept under control. Muddy boots should be left outside.*

*11.00a.m. - 2.30p.m. (3.00p.m. Saturday)*
*6.00p.m. - 11.00p.m.*
*Normal Sunday opening*

**Beers:** Six beers are normally on offer all changing regularly.
Fullers - London Pride is fairly permanent and the choice often
includes a dark mild.

## Terrain

A fair amount of peaceful lane walking with the rest of the walk equally
divided between woodland and open fields. There are no steep gradients
and all in all this is a very relaxed and pleasant walk.

## Getting to the Start (Grid Ref.018013)

The walk starts from The Bricklayers Arms which has a large car park.
Limited street parking is also possible. Probably the best way to approach
this remote pub is from the B4505 south of Hemel Hempstead and at
Bovingdon, take the road signposted to Chipperfield. At a crossroads turn
right in the direction of Flaunden and on entering Flaunden village turn left
at the first crossroads and you will arrive at The Bricklayers Arms.

## The Walk

(1) To start, facing the pub, turn right along the lane and when you arrive
at a lane leading off to your right signposted to Flaunden and Chenies,
turn left onto a signposted public footpath. Immediately after keep left
at a fork to follow the path uphill through woodland.

(2) At the far side of the wood go over a stile and turn right along a lane, ½ mile
passing the beautiful 'Hollow Hedge' on your left and continue until the
lane bends sharp right and leave it to join a track ahead, leading
through more woodland. Stay on the track, ignoring all turnings off and
much later, when it forks, keep left thereby maintaining your route
ahead. If at this point you find the going quite muddy, there is a
convenient path running parallel with the track on your left. Later the
track narrows to become a path and runs along the edge of a wood with
fields on your left, before eventually coming out into a field ahead.
Maintain your direction along the lefthand edge of the field to eventually
come out at a road at the village of Belsize.

(3) Cross the road and turn right along the pavement the other side to soon 1¼ miles
arrive at our second pub today, The Plough. Cross the road in front of
the pub and join Flaunden Lane thereby passing to the left of the pub
and later ignore a lane leading off to the right. Continue until you see a
signposted public footpath on your left and join this by going over a
stile. Proceed uphill along the righthand edge of a field and at the top
go over another stile and turn right along a lane

(4) Continue and at a T junction turn left along another lane (the one we 1¾ miles
were following earlier) and follow this for approximately ⅓ of a mile
until you see a signposted footpath on your right. After going up some
steps go over the stile and thereafter bear diagonally left across the
corner of a field. On meeting the edge of the field at the far side,
maintain your direction following the field edge with the hedge on your
right and at the field corner go over a stile onto a lane. Turn right along
the lane and after passing a farm on your right, join a fenced footpath

on your left running between fields. Later go over a stile and proceed diagonally right across a field ahead, heading for the far righthand corner. On reachlng the corner go over a stile into the field on your right and continue ahead along the field's lefthand edge.

2¾ miles **(5)** At the far slde of the field go over a stile and turn right along a lane and follow this down to a T junction. Turn left and retrace your steps

3 miles following the lane back to The Bricklayers Arms our starting point.

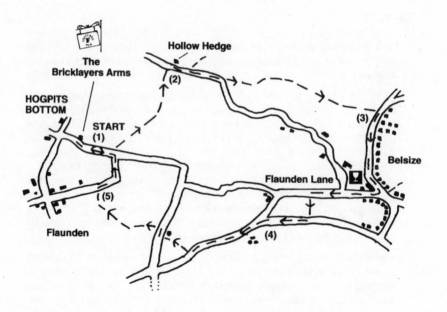

**Ordnance Survey Landranger Map 175**

# The Bull & Butcher - Turville

*Brakspear. Dating back to 1550, the white stuccoed facade of this pretty village pub belies a grisly event in its more recent history! In 1942 the landlord, Lacey Beckett, shot his wife, his dog and then himself in an upstairs room of the pub. In the public bar hangs a newspaper cutting dated 1942 relating the story, together with a photograph of Beckett. An old wooden shop sign on the wall indicates he was once a general dealer in the area. It is said that he does not rest easy in his grave and although no-one has seen his ghost he apparently makes his presence felt by talking to people! The name of the pub derives from Anne Boleyn who was also known as Nan Bullen, the butcher being Henry VIII, who finding that Anne Boleyn was not very good at producing a male heir, decided to have her beheaded! However, there is no trace whatsoever of the macabre evident today where you will only find good beer and an excellent choice of food with daily.specials, in comfortable surroundings. The pub is situated in the heart of the picturesque village, with a pleasant garden overlooked by a 17th century copstone windmill, featured in the film Chitty Chitty Bang Bang.*

✕ 🍴 ☂ **OPEN**    *1.00a.m. - 3.00p.m., 6.00p.m. -11.00p.m.*
                    *Normal Sunday opening*

**Beers:** Brakspears - Mild, Ordinary, Special Old –
all off beer engines

## Terrain

A lovely walk through valleys and over ridges along easy to follow paths. The scenery is some of the best the Chilterns can offer and particularly beautiful is the last stretch befor your final descent to the pub.

## Getting to the Start (Grid Ref.768911)

The walk starts from The Bull & Butcher pub at Turville. Apart from the car park there is limited roadside parking in the village itself so please be considerate to the local residents. Turville sits roughly in between Henley and High Wycombe. From the north take the turning signposted to Fingest from the B482 south of Stokenchurch and from Fingest, Turville is signposted. From the south, take the A4155 to Mill End and from there take the Hamble valley road to Fingest, then Turville.

## The Walk

**(1)** From the village centre, almost opposite the pub, take a track signposted as a public footpath beside the village post box. This passes between some pretty cottages, after which you should continue ahead uphill through a field heading for the windmill on top of Turville Hill. The windmill is famous for having featured in the film Chitty Chitty Bang Bang. At the far side of the field go over a couple of stiles in quick succession and maintain your route uphill along the righthand edge of a second field. As you climb there is a lovely view back over Turville and the Hamble valley. At the top of hill and at the far side of the field go over a stile ano turn right along a road and soon after, left, onto a signposted public footpath.

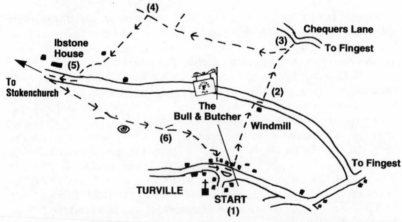

1/3 mile    **(2)** The footpath leads down the other eide of the hill through woodland and later, on meeting a fence ahead of you, go over a stile on your left to thereafter maintain your route downhill. Near the bottom the path breaks free of the wood and continues ahead through a field to arrive at a stile and gate.

3/4 mile    **(3)** Go over the stile and turn left along a bridleway which runs along the

*42*

bottom of a valley with Turville Hill on your left. Keep to the bridleway and the bottom of the valley, passing through a number of gates along the way to later meet a track onto which you should turn right, thereby maintaining the same direction. Keep to the track, ignoring any turnings off until you see a sign for Harecramp Estate, indicating a bridleway leading off to the left.

**(4)** Take this passing through a small gate beside the field gate and continue straight on uphill, between a series of wooden posts which at a certain time of the year holds a fence. Ahead to your right is the imposing Ibstone House. Halfway across the field pass to the left of an old barn, and at the far side pass through a gate to immediately after continue your climb, following a track which runs along the edge of a small wood. At the top of the hill the track passes through the grounds of Ibstone House on your right, before arriving at a road running along the top of the hill. — 1½ miles

**(5)** Turn right along the road with the walls to Ibstone House on your right and later take a signposted public footpath on the left, opposite the entrance to the house. The path runs gently down the side of Turville Hill, through woodland, your way being guided in places by yellow arrows on wooden posts. The path soon arrives at an area of mature beech wood where you should continue ahead going over a rough crossing track to soon after meet a prominent path at the edge of the wood where you should turn left along this. There is a fine view at first to your right over a typically beautiful Chiltern valley and you should follow the path for some distance until you see a well used path leading off to the right (take eare not to miss it). If you later find yourself following a track uphill you know you have missed the turning right. — 2 miles

**(6)** The path almost immedlately bends left to follow the edge of the wood and a fence to a field on your right. There are some more fine views over the valley on your right and ahead to your right, just visible, is Turville village. Further on you will meet a stile into a field on your right with a white topped post. Go over this and then bear gently left, not quite following the lefthand edge of the field and when visible, make for a stile ahead of you (there are two stiles along the field perimeter ahead, you should take the lower one and not the stile in the fields top lefthand corner). Go over the stile and follow a path which descends gradually, passing through a lovely area of natural chalk downland which gives way to woodland, after which the path ends at a stile. Go over the stile into a field, and turn sharp right to go over two stiles in quick succession into another field and thereafter follow a well used path across the centre of the field heading for Turville village. At the far side of the field go over a stile and down some steps to follow a path which runs alongside a converted flint and brick barn. Pass through a gate and turn left along a road through the centre of the village to shortly arrive back at the village green and The Bull & Butcher, our startlng point. — 2¾ miles

3 miles

# The Rising Sun
# - Little Hampton

*Freehouse. Built on the site of an old Roman settlement this building is partly converted from cottages which date from the 13th century and there are lower ceilings at the rear of the pub because of this. It became a pub in the mid 18th century and about ten years ago the whole pub was doubled in size by being extended as a mirror image of itself. The red brick which the pub is built of came from local brick kilns. Inside, the pub is light and airy with plaster and stripped pine walls. It has a brick and wooden beam bar and beamed ceilings. There are three rooms including a large restaurant area but food may be eaten anywhere in the pub. A green and patio at the front of the pub is popular with drinkers and diners alike in summer. A full, reasonably priced menu is available including daily specials and the desserts have earned a particularly good reputation. No dogs are allowed and muddy boots should be left in the entrance porch. Children are welcome and a suitable children's menu is available.*

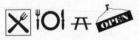

*11.30 a.m. - 3.00 p.m., 6.30 p.m. -11.00 p.m.*
*12.00 noon - 3.00 p.m. Sunday*
*Closed Sunday evenings and Monday lunchtimes except Bank Holidays.*

**Beers:**  Freehouse
Adnams Best Bitter
Three guest beers changed regularly, Mulled wine and hot spiced cider in winter and Sangria in summer.

## Terrain

Mainly undulating, in some cases fairly steep, through fields and along woodland paths. The woodland stretches are riddled with minor paths and care and a good sense of direction is required when walking these sections. This together with the fairly strenuous route is the reason why this walk is classed as Level C.

## Getting to the Start (Grid Ref.872043)

The walk starts from the Buckinghamshire County Council Cockshoots Picnic site at Cockshoots Wood. To get there take the A413 to Wendover Dean, 2 miles south of Wendover and there take a lane signposted to Coblers Hill. Approximately 1 mile distance along the lane on the left is the car park which is signposted.

## The Walk

(1) From the car park take the bridleway, marked with a blue arrow, into Cockshoots Wood. This leads gently uphill, running parallel with the lane on your right, before bending left and climbing more steeply. A short time after, turn right onto a path marked by a white arrow and thereafter follow the path uphill through the wood, ignoring all turnings off and continuing to be guided by the white arrows. Later, as the path begins to level out, you will see a marked crossing path (white arrows). Ignore this carrying straight on along the main path which continues to be marked by white arrows. A few metres on you will arrive at a T junction in the form of a track, onto which you should turn right. A few paces on where the track forks, keep left, and shortly after on meeting a crossing track, continue straight on. A few paces after this, ignore a path forking off to the left, thereby maintaining your route ahead, keeping right where the track later forks again, to arrive at a wide track in front of a cottage. Turn right along the track to shortly arrive at a lane.

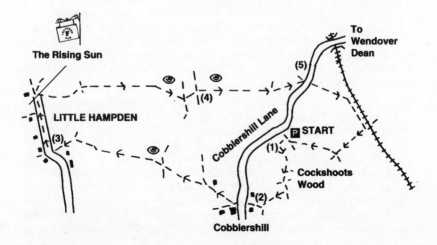

½ mile   **(2)** Cross the lane and join a track the other side marked as the South Bucks Way. A short time on, on meeting a couple of houses on your right, go over a stile on your left, through a small field and over another stile, then straight across the second field in the direction of the South Bucks Way arrow. At the far side of the field go over a stile and follow a narrow path downhill through scrub to eventually arrive at a stile near the bottom of a valley. Go over the stile and maintain your route ahead along the righthand edge of a field and at the far side and at the bottom of the valley, go over a crossing track and maintain your direction, now following the lefthand edge of the field ahead on your right. At the far side of the field do not pass through the gate ahead but instead take a path slightly to your right which winds uphill through woodland to eventually meet a wide track. Turn left along the track in the direction of the white arrow to shortly meet a lane.

1¼ miles   **(3)** Turn right along the lane to eventually arrive at The Rising Sun pub. The lane finishes at the pub and here you should take a track forking off to the right and immediately after, turn right again to join a signposted public footpath leading steeply downhill through woodland. Keep to the path being guided by the white arrows, to eventually come out at a wide track near the bottom. Go over this, and maintain your route ahead, now following a track along the lefthand edge of a field. At the far side of the field follow the track left into a wood and immediately upon entering the wood, turn right, to follow a track uphill, thereby maintaining your original direction. The climb out of the valley can be quite tough going, especially if you have enjoyed the food and drink at The Rising Sun. Near the top go over a crossing path and follow a narrow path ahead, to shortly arrive at a track.

2 miles   **(4)** Turn left along the track and after a few paces, right, to go over a stile into a field. Proceed along the lefthand edge of the field descending into the Missenden valley. At the far side of the field the path naturally joins a track which continues to descend along the edge of a second field. Approximately three quarters of the way across the field, go over a stile on your left, across a horse gallop and over a second stile. Turn immediately rlight to follow the gallop and continue until you see a stile on your right. Go over this and back across the horse gallop and over another stile onto a lane.

2½ miles   **(5)** Cross the lane, go over a stile the other side and proceed along the righthand edge of a small field to shortly cross another stile and continue along the edge of a second field. When the field edge does a sharp 'V'-like turn at the far side, continue ahead and a few paces on turn right, now following the lefthand field edge with the Aylesbury to London railway line running parallel on your left. Leave the field at the far corner to turn right onto a track and follow this uphill heading for Cockshoots Wood. On entering the wood, take a marked footpath right. Follow this through the wood until you arrive at a T junction where you should turn right onto another path going downhill, to soon come out at

3 miles   the car park where we started.

# 𝕿𝖍𝖊 𝖂𝖍𝖎𝖙𝖊 𝕳𝖆𝖗𝖙
# - 𝖀𝖕𝖕𝖊𝖗 𝕾𝖚𝖓𝖉𝖔𝖓

*Charles Wells. There has been a pub where The White Hart now stands since the time of the plague when people, trying to escape from the effects of the plague in London began to settle in Upper Sundon. However, the building is much newer having been razed to the ground by fire and rebuilt earlier this century. It is now an attractive pub with a green at the front. A landlady in the 19th century, so the story goes, committed suicide by throwing herself down the well which is now beneath the kitchen. There are rumours that she still makes her presence felt from time to time! The lounge bar is comfortably furnished and carpeted in traditional style and to the rear of the pub is a garden where games are provided. A bar menu is available at lunchtime and evenings serving traditional pub food. Dogs and children are welcome.*

 *11.00a.m.-11.00p.m.*
*Normal Sunday opening*

**Beers:**   Charles Wells - Bombardier, Eagle
Guest Beer

47

## Terrain

Mainly flat through wide open fields. The final stretches along the top of the Sundon Hills afford magnificent views over the Bedfordshire countryside.

## Getting to the Start (Grid Ref.047286)

The walk starts from the car park for the Sundon Hills Country Park. This is situated on the road between Upper Sundon and Harlington. It is only a 3 mile drive from junction 12 of the M1 and there is a railway station at Harlington only 2 miles away.

## The Walk

**(1)** To start, walk out of the car park, turn right along the road and after approximately 50 metres pass through a gate on your left into a field, following the sign for the Icknield Way. Proceed along the lefthand edge of the field with fine views to your right over Bedfordshire and continue until you meet a line of trees almost at the far side. Turn right here and follow the line of trees in the direction of the Icknield Way arrow and on reaching the field perimeter, turn left to soon arrive at a gate on your right.

½ mile

**(2)** Do not pass through the gate but instead leave the Icknield Way by bearing diagonally left across the field in the direction of a bridleway arrow. At the far corner pass through a gate and turn left along a track, heading for the houses of Upper Sundon. The track eventually arrives at Upper Sundon beside The Red Lion pub, though this is not our featured pub.

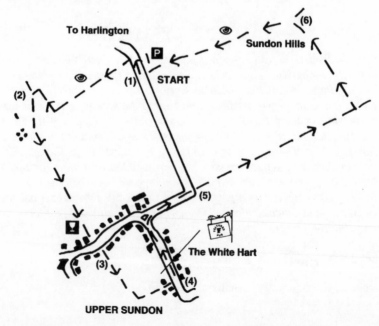

*48*

**(3)** Cross the road and go over a stile the other side to join a signposted footpath across the centre of a field. Approximately $\frac{2}{3}$ of the way across, bear left, heading for a stile at the lefthand perimeter. To help guide you, a wide shallow ditch lined with a few straggly bushes, leads down to the stile. Go over the stile and walk through a car park to come out beside The White Hart, our featured pub.

1½ miles

**(4)** After the pub, turn left along the road and at a T junction turn right in the direction of the sign for Harlington. Follow the road out of the village and shortly after, where it bends sharp left, leave it to join a signposted public footpath ahead.

1¾ miles

**(5)** The footpath proceeds along the righthand edge of a very large field. When you eventually reach the corner at the far side, turn left to continue along the field edge, heading for the scarp slope of the Sundon Hills.

2 miles

**(6)** On almost reaching the second corner of the field, go over a stile on your right and thereafter turn left to follow a track around a small coombe with a fence on your left, to shortly arrive at a field gate. Pass through a kissing gate to your left and then bear left, keeping a fence on your left, to follow a path along the top of the Sundon Hills, enjoying fine views to your right over the Bedfordshire countryside all the way back to the car park. our starting point.

2½ miles

3 miles

# The Crooked Billet
## - Stoke Row

*Brakspear. The Crooked Billet enjoys a beautiful position tucked away on a narrow lane on the outskirts of the village and surrounded by fields and woodland. The pub with its white walls, attic windows and green shutters makes a pretty picture. The building was built in 1642 as a smallholding and sold its first beer in 1750. The large room at the end of the pub, which is now used as a dining room and sometimes as a function room, was used to house the cherry pickers who came to pick cherries in the cherry orchard to finance the Maharajah's Well at Stoke Row. At the end of the 18th century the building was used by bodgers (woodworkers) and this use continued until 1960.*

*Today The Crooked Billet offers the finest food you will eat at any pub anywhere. Unusually for a pub it has no bar but there are three separate rooms where you may sit to drink and eat. Should you not be hungry enough to eat a three course meal then you are encouraged to try one of the delicious starters as a light meal. The largest room has a brick and wood fireplace, lit in winter. Bookshelves line one of the walls and there are interesting old portraits on another. The middle room has musical instruments, decorative plates and rural pictures to enhance the pub's rusticity The small room at the entrance has a quarry tiled floor and Inglenook fireplace; a wine rack and large baskets add decoration. There are tables outside In the garden at the front of the pub. Food is served every day lunchtime and evenings and the menus are changed weekly. At least once a month a menu is offered which consists exclusively of local products from within a 10 mile radius. The pub also produces its own honey which is for sale. You're quite likely to find the odd stray chicken running around outside too, all of which adds to the appeal of this charming rustic pub.*

     12.00 noon- 3.00pm., 700pm -11.00p.m.
12.00 noon- 10.30p.m. Sunday

**Beers:**  Brakspears - Ordinary, Special. O B J

## Terrain
An undulating walk through fields and along woodland paths. Compared to many other parts of the Chilterns, the paths followed in this walk remain relatively unexplored therefore a peaceful day out is almost guaranteed.

## Getting to the Start (Grid Ref.677841)
The walk starts from the Maharajah's Well at the centre of Stoke Row. Roadside parking is possible but please be considerate of the local residents The best way to approach the village is to take the B481 to Highmoor just south of Nettlebed and from there Stoke Row is signposted being approximately two miles along a lane west.

*The colourful Maharajah's Well was built in 1863 and was a gift from the Maharajah of Benares. The well which is just 4 feet wide was dug by hand to a depth of 368 feet, quite an achievement.*

## The Walk
**(1)** Facing the Maharajah's Well, turn right along the road and continue until you arrive at The Farmer Inn. Turn left into the narrow Knottwood Lane and follow it gently downhill, passing some pretty cottages, to later arrive at the Crooked Billet.

**(2)** Continue past the pub and a few metres on turn left onto a tarmac drive    ½ mile
which leads downhill and just before the entrance to Bush Wood House, turn right onto a wide path. The path leads downhill through woodland and you must ignore all turnings off to eventually arrive at a very narrow lane at the bottom of a valley. Cross the lane and join a signposted bridleway the other side, slightly to your right and follow this uphill to meet a second lane. Cross the lane and join a track the other side which follows the perimeter fencing to a property on your left. Keep to the track, once again ignoring all turnings off, to later pass a couple of properties on your right. Immediately after these go over a stile on your right beside a field gate into a field.

**(3)** Go gently diagonally left across the field and as you reach the centre,    1¼ miles
head for a stile visible the other side Go over two stiles in quick succession, then bear diagonally left across the next field, going downhill, heading for the far lefthand corner. At the field corner, and at the bottom of a valley, go over a stile beside a gate and continue up the other side, bearing gently diagonally left to reach another stile beside a

farm gate at the top of the field. Go over the stile and continue ahead along the leftand edge of another field. At the far side go over a stile, then across part of a smaller field and over yet another stile to thereafter follow a narrow path ahead through a strip of woodland, including laurels, to eventually arrive at a crossing path beside a converted barn

1½ miles **(4)** Turn right along the crossing path marked by a white arrow and as path H3, and pass to the left of the converted barn before arriving at an iron gate. Pass through the gate and continue in the direction of a yellow footpath arrow to join the drive to the converted barn and another property. After a few paces turn right passing through another gate into a field, now following a path marked as H6. On entering the field, turn right to follow the field edge and at the far corner go over a stile and continue in the same direction across the next field. As you near the corner of the field look out for and go over a stile on your right and then turn immediately left to follow the lefthand edge of another field. Pass to the right of a concrete carcass of an old barn and continue ahead to the field corner. Go over a stile beside a farm gate and maintain your route ahead along the lefthand edge of the next field. At the field corner go over a stile and follow a narrow path ahead. This leads naturally onto a drive which you should follow between the first houses of the hamlet of Witheridge Hill to arrive at a "T" junction.

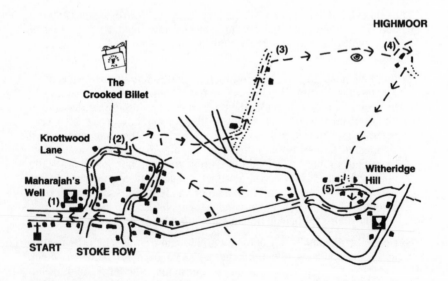

**(5)** Turn left and then almost immediately right across a small grass area 2 miles to thereafter follow a narrow footpath downhill. The path follows a garden hedge on your left to shortly arrive at a track onto which you should turn left to meet a lane. Our way is right, downhill, along the lane but a short detour left (up the lane and first right beside the old School House) will bring you to another good pub on this walk, the Rising Sun, which boasts a menu of 40 dishes. To continue follow the lane downhill to a junction of roads where you should ignore the first lane on your right to turn right instead at the T junction, in the direction of the signpost for Stoke Row, Checkendon and Ipsden. Keep to the righthand side of the road and after approximately 20 metres turn right onto a track leading to a property on your right and immediately after joining, turn left onto another track leading gently uphill through woodland. Keep to the track, ignoring any turnings off, which later narrows to become a path where you should maintain your route ahead, still ignoring any turnings off. Please ensure you do not take any of the paths to the right. As you near the far side of the wood, the path arrives at a "T" junction where you should turn right to follow a path along the edge of the wood with fields on your left. Once again, keep to the path, ignoring any turnings off, to eventually arrive at a lane. At this point take care not to take a marked path leading right downhill. Instead join the lane and turn left, following it uphill between the houses of Stoke Row. The lane twists before arriving at a crossroads beside the village green. Turn right at the crossroads to follow the road in the direction of the signs for Nuffield and Ipsden, back to the Maharajah's Well, our starting point. $3^1/_4$ miles

# The Fox Inn
# - Dunsmore

*Freehouse. There are rumours that Dick Turpin used to visit The Fox which was originally called The Bugle Horn and was on the stage coach run. It is the highest pub in the Chilterns and being close to Chequers was used by Harold Wilson and Ted Heath in the days when security could afford to be more relaxed. The building has lime and lava walls and was converted from cottages in the middle of the last century. It is beautifully situated being tucked away at the end of a narrow lane. Inside is a small bar which opens into a large conservatory garden room. The bar has a red quarry tiled floor and at one end is a brick fireplace. Country style furniture, horse brasses and decorative plates enhance the cosy atmosphere. Outside is a very pleasant, large, lawned garden which has seating for 200 and above the conservatory is a delightful fox pub sign. A full home cooked menu is provided as well as bar snacks and a barbecue is held every Sunday lunchtime, weather permitting.*

*11.00 a.m. - 3.00 p.m. summer.*
*Close at 2.30 p.m.winter, 6.30 p.m. - 11.00 p.m*
*Closed Sunday and Monday evenings and closes at 10.30 p.m. in Winter Monday to Friday but 11.00p.m. on Saturdays.*

**Beers:**   Tring Brewery - Ridgeway Ale
Wadsworth - 6X
Guest Beer - changed weekly

## Terrain
Flat walking nearly all along woodland paths which in wet weather can get very muddy. The highlight of the walk apart from the pub, is the summit of Coombe Hill from where there are incredible views.

## Getting to the Start (Grid Ref.862053)
The walk starts from a large parking area near Coombe Hill. The car park is on a lane which services Dunsmore between the A413 and the road that skirts Chequers from Butlers Cross. The lane can be joined from the A413 approximalely 1 mile south of Wendover where it is signposted to Dunsmore. Follow the lane through Dunsmore and just over a mile after the village as the lane bends sharp left, you will see the parking area on your right. Alternatively, at Butler's Cross, on the B4010, take the road south, signposted to Great Missenden and after just over a mile, take a lane left signposted to Dunsmore. Continue until the lane bends sharp right and you will see the car park ahead of you.

## The Walk
(1) To start, walk through the length of the car park in the direction of a public bridleway sign. At the end of the car park, pass through a kissing gate ahead to your left and immediately after, ignore a path on your left, instead following a path ahead through woodland with a fence on your rIght. Keep to the main path which continues to run parallel with a fence, ignorIng all turnings off, to eventually pass through a kissing gate at the edge of the wood.

(2) Turn left, passing a National Trust sign for Coombe Hill and thereafter continue to bear left, keeping close to the perimeter of the wood on your left. When the wood on your left ends, continue ahead across open grass hillside, making for the large monument at the top of Coombe Hill. Coombe Hill is 257 metres above sea level and almost the highest point in the Chilterns. The monument, erected in 1804 commemorates the men of Buckinghamshire who lost their lives fighting in the Boer War. ¼ mile

(3) To continue, as you arrive at the monument, bear gently left, now following the white acorns of the Ridgeway, along a path which hugs the side of the hill. Do not make the mistake of following the path that runs along the very top of the hill, instead take the one very slightly further down to the right. The path eventually bends left, leaving the open grass hillside, to arrive at a kissing gate on your right. Pass through this and thereafter follow a path through woodland, being guided by the white acorns, to eventually arrive at a lane. ½ mile

(4) Turn right along the lane and after approximately 50 metres turn left at a Ridgeway signpost, and after a few paces along a track, go over the second stile on your right, marked by a white acorn, to follow a well worn path through more woodland. Later, go over a stile on your right 1 mile

and then turn left onto another path, still following the white acorns. Continue until you arrive at a signposted crossing path and here leave the Ridgeway by taking the path left. Make sure you do not miss this. The path, though less prominent than the Ridgeway is easy to follow, being well marked by yellow arrows. Keep to the path, being careful to follow the arrows, ignoring all turnings off, including at one point a marked crossing path and some time after this a marked path off to the right, to after approximately $^3/_4$ mile come out at a lane running through the centre of the wood.

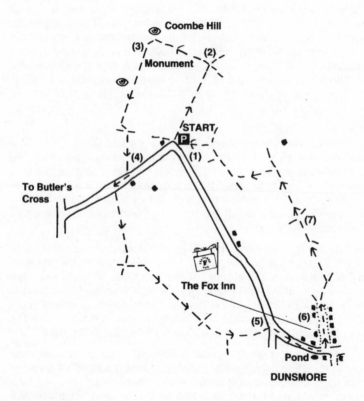

2 miles  **(5)** Turn right along the lane and follow it uphill, ignoring another lane on the right, leading to Dunsmore Livery Stables. At the top of the hill the lane enters Dunsmore village. Follow the lane past the village pond and immediately after, turn left onto another lane signposted Dunsmore Village Only. Follow the lane for approximately 100 metres and you will arrive at The Fox Inn.

56

**(6)** From The Fox, maintain your direction along the lane, though now it is signposted as no access for cars and as a public bridleway. When the tarmac ends. follow a track ahead and ignore a signposted footpath on the left. A short distance further, leave the track to join a fenced footpath on the left, marked by a yellow arrow and accessed by way of a stile. Stay on the fenced path, ignoring all turnings off, until you eventually arrive at a track wlth a cattle grid on your right. 2¼ miles

**(7)** Maintain your route ahead going over the track with the fence still on your right but with a bank (the parish boundary) now on your left. After a short distance, turn left onto a path marked by a yellow arrow. Make sure you do not miss this and follow the path, being guided by the regularly spaced yellow arrows on the trees. Ignore any turnings off to soon arrive at a grass crossing path marked by yellow arrows. Turn right onto the crossing path and, once again, follow the yellow arrows and ignore all turnings off until you meet a path leading off to the left, marked by an arrow (this is in fact a crossing path but the arrow just points left). Turn left onto the path and follow it, being guided by the yellow arrows, back to the car park and our starting point. 2¾ miles

3¼ miles

# The Old Plough
# - West Wycombe

*Freehouse. This pub is situated in the centre of the splendidly picturesque High Street with its many old buildings. The National Trust own most of the village including the 17th century building which houses The Old Plough. One unusual feature is that it has an upstairs lounge bar which leads out on to a sloping garden built into the hillside. A public bar is to the right of the entrance downstairs. Stepping into this pub is like stepping back into history and its historic atmosphere is almost tangible. It has half wood panelled walls in the lounge bar with a blue carpet and blue upholstered seats. Special events are chalked on the wooden beams such as the Folk Club which is held every Wednesday. Anyone brave enough can volunteer to perform their party piece at this weekly event. A corner bookshelf with a few well worn popular novels together with copper and brass bric-a-brac and a brick fireplace complete the decor. An extensive bar menu is available with daily specials listed on a blackboard, serving snacks and reasonably priced meals. The lounge bar is closed Sunday evenings and all day Monday. When the bar is open seating is also available in the garden. No children are allowed in the bar after 8.00 p.m. and dogs are welcome provided they are kept under control.*

 *11.30a.m.- 2.30p.m.Monday to Friday*
*5.30 p.m. - 11.00 p.m. Monday to Friday*
*All day Saturday. Normal Sunday opening*

**Beers:** A choice of three of the following at any one time plus beers from the Rebellion Beer Company. A choice of 10 beers over a 2½ week period
Adnams - Bitter
Burton - Bitter
Greene King - Abbot Ale
Tetley- Bitter
Wadsworth - 6X

## Terrain
Mainly through fields and along woodland paths. There are a couple of climbs on the second leg, quite steep, but nothing very difficult. In summer it is worth making time to visit West Wycombe House and the Hell Fire Caves below West Wycombe Hill.

## Getting to the Start (Grid Ref.826947)
The walk starts from the public car park beside the West Wycombe Garden Centre. The car park and Garden Centre is signposted from the A40 at West Wycombe and is off the road to Bledlow Ridge.

## The Walk
**(1)** To start, leave the car park and turn right along the lane towards the A40. At the A40 turn right and follow it in the direction of the sign for Oxford. You will soon pass the old pound on your right, used for enclosing stray animals. Follow the A40 which at this point is bordered by some lovely red beech, until you see a signposted public footpath on your right, this is just after passing the entrance of Towerage Lane on the left.

**(2)** Go over a stile and follow a footpath diagonally left across the centre of ¼ mile a field. To your right now at the top of West Wycombe hill you will see the tower of St. Lawrence Church, easily identifiable by its golden ball and behind, are good views to West Wycombe House. At the far side of the field, pass through a gap in the hedge and maintain your direction across the centre of another field passing between some electricity pylons. At the far side of this field, the path leads naturally into another field. If in doubt, follow the direction of a white arrow on a fence post on your right and once again maintain your direction, now walking along the lefthand edge of a field, with a hedge on your left. The route begins to level out and as you near the far side of the field veer slightly right and follow the field edge round, with Great Cockshoots Wood bordering the field on your left. Do not take the first track into the wood (as a guide, this one is approximately 15 metres in from the field corner) but continue round for approximately a further 50 metres until you see a stile on your left with a track entering the wood just to its right. Please note the stile can be quite hidden in summer, so take care not to miss it.

**(3)** Go over the stile and follow a path marked by white lines and arrows on ¾ mile trees, through Cockshoots Wood. The path goes over a number of

*59*

crossing tracks and you should ignore any other turnings off, keeping to the marked path, to eventually come out at a sunken track at the far side of the wood. Turn right along the track, going uphill, and after a few paces when the track forks, maintain your direction by taking the righthand fork. The track leads over the top of the hill and down the other side, being quite steep in places, to eventually end at the bottom of a valley where it meets a lane beside the heautiful Chorley Farmhouse.

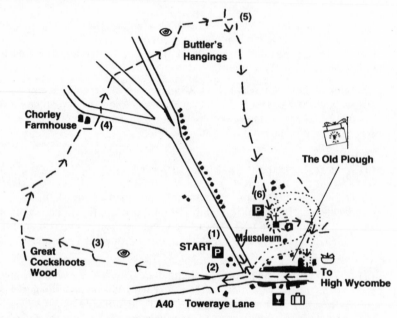

1½ miles  **(4)** Cross the lane and go over a stile beside a gate the other side and follow a grass track ahead along the lefthand edge of a field. To your right you will again see the tower of St. Lawrence Church. After passing between the same line of electricity pylons we met earlier, go over a stile at the far side and cross a lane to go over another stile and thereafter, follow a path ahead between fields. At the far side go over another stile and cross a second lane and then once again, a stile the other side to thereafter follow a hedged path between fields, going gently uphill. Pass through a gate to enter Buttler's Hangings, a nature reserve run by BBONT. There is an information sign at the side of the path on your right. Follow the path uphill through scrub (at a fork keep left) to shortly arrive at an area of natural chalk grassland where there are some magnificent views over the earlier part of our walk. Continue to climb to later pass through a gate into an area of mature woodland. Follow the path ahead, passing to the right of a number of small pits and continue. ignoring any turnings off, until you come out at a crossing track, just before a new plantation.

**(5)** Turn right along the crossing track to after a short distance, meet another track onto which you should turn right. This track can, in wet weather, be very muddy and therefore to avoid the mud I advise you to follow a path running parallel to the track on the right. Follow the track along the top of a hill, ignoring any turnings off, to eventually come out at the grass car park at top of West Wycombe Hill.

2½ miles

**(6)** Leave the track, bearing right across the car park, heading for the church. At the far side of the car park pass through a gate into the churchyard and follow the path to the church entrance beneath the tower. *Of medieval origin 18th century alterations by Sir Francis Dashwood make this period unrecognisable. The golden ball on top of the tower is said to be a copy of the Ball of Fortune In Venlce. For a small fee it is sometimes possible to climb the tower.* Thereafter follow the concrete path through the churchyard passing to the left of the church to shortly come out onto open hillside beside the Dashwood Mausoleum. A short detour right along another path will allow you to have a better view of the mausoleum. For historical notes on the mausoleum see under The Red Lion Bradenham. As the concrete path ends, maintain your direction down the side of the hill as though making for the A40 and High Wycombe now in view directly ahead. Go over a crossing path and continue your descent, ignorlng any further turnings off to, after passing through some wooden rails, arrive at a narrow lane. Turn right along the lane and after a short distance fork left along Church Lane, to enter West Wycombe village. This is probably the best way to enter West Wycombe through a quiet back street of beautiful traditional cottages. The entrance ends by passing beneath an arch of the 15th century Church Loft to come out at the A40 underneath a large Clock. *The church loft was originally built as a rest house for pilgrims. Over the years part of the building has also acted as the village lock up.* Turn right along the main street to shortly arrive at our featured pub, The Old Plough. After the pub, continue along the main street to arrive at the turning signposted to Bedlow on your right. Take this and retrace your steps to the Garden Centre car park.

3 miles

3¼ miles

**Ordnance Survey Landranger Map 175**

# The Stag and Huntsman - Hambleden

*Freehouse. Set in a small peaceful village this attractive flint stone and brick tile hung pub dates back to the mid 17th century and has been used as a film set. Inside there is a public bar at the front of the pub with the lounge bar at the rear with windows overlooking the garden. There is also a separate restaurant. However food can be ordered from the bar where there is a blackboard menu with additions to the varied menu in the evening. The lounge bar has a peaceful cosy country pub atmosphere with pictures of hunting and country scenes horse brasses and other items of brass and copper adding to the ambience. There is comfortable bench seating as well as separate tables and chairs in this cosy carpeted room which features a brick fireplace. Bed and breakfast is also available here.*

  *11-00a.m. - 3.00p.m., 6.00p.m. - 11.00p.m.*

**Beers:** Brakspears - Ordinary, Special
Chiltern Valley - Old Luxters Barn Ale
Wadsworth - 6X
Guest Beer - changed regularly

## Terrain
A beautiful walk following field and woodland paths. There is one fairly steep ascent at the start to climb out of the Hamble valley but otherwise the going is fairly easy. Some of the paths can heeome a little overgrown in summer so think twice before wearing those shorts!

## Getting to the Start (Grid Ref.785866)
The walk starts from the public car park at Hambleden. To get there take the A4155 in between Marlow and Henley and at Mill End, take the road signposted to Hambleden and Fingest. After approximately 1 mile turn right into Hambleden village and follow the road past The Stag and Huntsman to reach the public car park.

## The Walk
(1) From the car park walk to its entrance, then turn right away from The Stag and Huntsman pub up a narrow lane marked 'Private - Access Only'. After a short distance, turn right onto a track signposted as a public footpath and follow this until you see an entrance to a field on your left. Turn left here but do not enter the field, instead follow a narrow path marked by a white arrow which leads uphill following the field fence. This path is not always easy to find so take care you do not miss it. As you climb there are some lovely views right, across to the Thames valley. The path later continues to climb through a beech wood and further on passes through a rough clearing, in the centre of which it meets a junction of tracks. Go over the first track and a few paces after, turn left, onto another track, keeping your eyes open for and following the white arrows painted on trees. After approximately 20 metres turn right onto a narrow path and go over a stile inlo a field.

(2) Carry straight on along the lefthand edge of the field and when this ½ mile bends sharp left, continue ahead bearing very gently right across the centre of the field. As you near the centre, head for some gates visible at the far side. Pass through the gates and go over a track to follow a grass track ahead through fields, making for the houses and farm buildings of Rotten Row, visible ahead.

(3) On meeting a lane turn left and follow it to soon enter the hamlet of Rotten Row. Follow the lane past the village pond and iust after, as it bends left, leave it and continue ahead to pass through a metal gate into a field. Cross the field in the direction of the footpath sign and at the far side, go over a stile and cross a second field in thc same direction. As you near the centre, head for stile beside a gate at the far side. Cross the stile and soon after, a second stile and thereafter turn left along a lane.

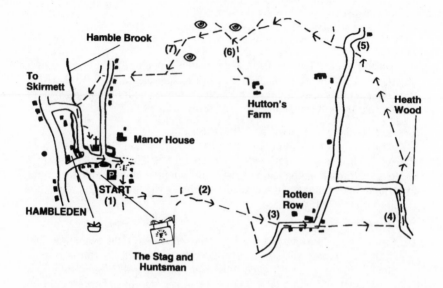

Hamble Brook

To
Skirmett

(7)

(6)

(5)

Hutton's
Farm

Heath
Wood

Manor House

START

(1)

(2)

Rotten
Row

(3)

(4)

HAMBLEDEN

The Stag and
Huntsman

1 mile   **(4)** Follow the lane for some distance until it bends sharp left and at this point, leave it by passing through a one barred gate ahead onto a tarmac chip parking area. Keep to the righthand edge of the parking area and after approximately 20 metres, turn right onto a narrow path marked by a white arrow and a number 7. The path leads downhill through woodland and just as it begins to rise again, turn left onto another path marked by a white arrow. Later go over a crossing path to soon after this, arrive at a track. Cross the track and go over a stile and bear diagonally right across a field. On nearing the far side, continue ahead along the lefthand field edge, now heading for a stile directly in front of you. Cross the stile and follow a narrow path along the edge of a wood and after a short distance look out for a stile on your left. Cross this and a second immediately after, to then continue along the righthand edge of a field. The field edge slowly curves right and just before the curve ends turn left across the field heading for a stile at the far side.

1½ miles   **(5)** Go over the stile, cross a lane and go over another stile the other side, slightly to your right, to thereafter follow a wide path through woodland. Ignore any turnings off and keep to the main path which eventually leads to an area of newly planted woodland. The path passes through this bearing gently left. to later arrive at a wide track. Maintain your route ahead along the track to shortly meet a second track onto which you should turn left. thereby still maintaining the same direction. The track passes through another area of newly planted woodland and here, there are some lovely views on your right across the Hamble valley. Just as the woodland ends and the track Continues between fields, turn right onto a narrow path marked by some white arrows on a tree (if you find yourself following a track between fields you know you have missed the turning).

1¾ miles

**(6)** The path starts a gradual descent into the Hamble valley, but after a short distance you should take a path on your left marked by a white arrow which leads along the top of the valley side. Make sure you do not miss this as it is a long climb back up the hill to find it. The view to your right is of the hamlet of Pheasants Hill. Later the path bends left in the direction of a white arrow on a wooden post to enter a field. Do not make the mistake of following another narrower path ahead.

2½ miles

**(7)** The path makes a straight and prominent line across the field, passing over a ridge from the top of which there are lovely views ahead towards the Thames Valley. At the far side of the field go over a stile and then right along a track. The track leads down to a lane between some pretty flint and brick cottages. Cross the lane and pass through a kissing gate the other side into a lovely meadow at the bottom of the Hamble valley. Turn left and follow a path which bears to the right of the church (not left). At the other side of the meadow pass through a kissing gate and turn left along the lane, heading for Hambleden Church. Take the path through the churchyard and on reaching the church entrance, turn right to follow the path between an avenue of neatly cut yews and pass through the lychgate to arrive at the village centre with its much photographed water pump. *Hambleden is one of the best preserved villages in the Chilterns. The Manor House was once home to the Earl of Cardigan of "The Charge of the Light Brigade" fame. It is now home to the W. H. Smith family Viscounts Hambleden who made their fortune through their famous chain of stationery and book shops. The church is well worth a visit and the village's pretty streets are fun to explore. The village may look familiar even if you have never visited before. This is probably due to the village having been the setting for many a period film or T.V. drama.* Turn left and follow the road to The Stag and Huntsman, after which it is only a short stagger back to the car park, our starting point.

3¼ miles

# The Stonor Arms
## - Stonor

*Freehouse. Set in a peaceful village The Stonor Arms adjoins the Stonor Park estate. Built in the mid 18th century it was originally a convent school attached to Stonor House but has been a pub for the past 120 years and is now a fine country house hotel offering accommodation in 9 en-suite rooms. It has an elegant restaurant with its own pretty conservatory serving an imaginative a la carte menu. The conservatory overlooks the well maintained garden. The bar has flagstone floors antique furniture and a comfortable settee and chairs. An interesting display of rowing regalia adorn the walls including a jacket, caps, oars and old photographs of rowing crews. There is a fireplace with a wooden mantle and wooden beams and rugs on the stone floor all help to give a delightful country house atmosphere. A bar menu is available offering a full range of snacks. No dogs are allowed and it is requested that muddy boots are removd before entering*

      *12.00 - 2.00 p.m. 6.00 p.m. - 11.00 p.m.*
*12.00noon-2.00p.m.*
*7.00 p.m. -10.30 p.m. Sunday*

**Beers:**   Chiltern Valley- Old Luxtors Barn Ale
             Wadsworth - IPA

**Terrain**

Mainly woodland paths with, at one point, a fair amount of lane walking. There are two fairly strenuous ascents so the walk is not for the unfit.

Part of the walk meets the route for The Crown, Pishill.

**Gettings to the Start (Grid Ref.721878)**

The walk starts from the BBONT car park at the Warburg Nature Reserve. This is quite remote and care must be taken not to take the wrong turning. The easiest way to get there is to join the B480 from the A423 north of Henley and after passing through Middle Assenden, take a narrow lane left signposted to Bix Bottom. This is easy to miss so take care. Follow the lane for approximately 2 miles, ignoring all turnings off, to reach the car park whlch is on your right. The car park has a gate which is often shut but not locked.

**The Walk**

(1) From the car park walk out of the entrance by which you arrived and turn left along a track. After a few paces turn left again onto a signposted footpath. Follow this uphill where as you progress, there are some excellent views back over the reserve. Near the top ignore a stile on your left and continue to eventually reach a track marked as The Oxfordshire Way.

(2) Turn left along the track and after a few paces, right and just before ¼ mile you enter a farmyard, turn left again onto a signposted footpath. Just after entering a field turn right and follow a path diagonally right across the centre. As you cross the field there are marvellous views to your right across to the hills in Berkshire. At the far side of the field go over a stile and follow a narrow path through a beech wood. After a

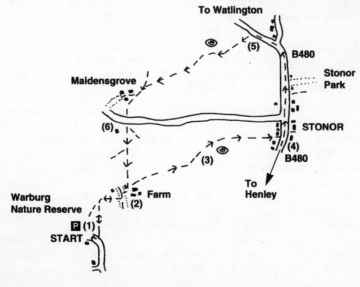

67

few paces the path joins a track and you should carry straight on in the direction of the white arrows, following the track downhill through the wood.

1 mile **(3)** At the far side of the wood go over a stile to enter a field where you are immediately rewarded with excellent views across the Stonor valley and immediately below to Stonor itself, beyond which is Stonor House. Carry straight on across the centre of the field, making for the village below. At the far side go over another stile and maintain your direction across a second field. Go over another stile and follow a narrow fenced path to soon meet the B480 at Stonor. Turn right along the road and you will soon arrive at The Stonor Arms.

1½ miles **(4)** From the pub our way is, at first, to retrace our steps along the road but this time you should ignore the footpath on your left by which we arrived and continue to follow the road out of the village, ignoring a lane leading off to the left. It is not long before you pass the entrance to Stonor Park on the right and if you have time and the park is open it is well worth breaking here to enjoy a visit to the house. Stay on the road, past Stonor Park and later ignore a lane leading off to the right and shortly after this (approximately 75 metres) leave the road and take a signposted footpath on the left signposted to Maidensgrow.

2¼ miles **(5)** The footpath runs uphill in between thick hedges, some of which can be a little overgrown. If this is the case it is possible to follow the lefthand edge of the field on your right to rejoin the correct path at the top of the field. Higher up the hill the path enters Pishillbury Wood and from here the path is well defined as well as being marked by white arrows on the trees. As you meander through the wood you occasionally get an excellent view right, through the upper stretches of the valley towards Pishill. Eventually the path levels out and not long after, you arrive at a 'T' junction in the form of another path (marked as path PS17 and with white arrows on a tree). Turn left onto the path which soon starts a gentle descent. At a fork keep left, passing to the left of some houses to descend quite steeply through a wood of beech and holly before arriving at a narrow lane.

2¾ miles **(6)** Cross the lane and follow a marked bridleway the other side (ignore a track which forks left) and follow this uphill along the edge of the wood, ignoring all further turnings off to reach the far side. Here you must ignore a stile and footpath on your right, and maintain your route ahead to leave the wood and enter a field. Continue straight across the field making for the rooftops of the farm ahead. On nearing the far corner you will see a path on your left, re-crossing the field, you will probably recognise this as the one we took earlier on our way to Stonor. Unless you started at the pub in which case turn left and read from the second sentence paragraph (2), do not join the path but continue ahead to follow the first part of our route in reverse, back to the car park at the
3¼ miles bottom of the valley and the Warburg Nature Reserve.

*68*

# The Anglers Retreat
# - Marsworth

*Freehouse. The Anglers Retreat is a very old pub, dating back to the 16th century. It is close to the Grand Union Canal where fishermen are usually to be seen patiently waiting for a catch and the pub has a decidedly fishy feel about it (the wet kind, not dubious!) in accordance with its name! It is furnished in traditional style with an L shaped carpeted bar and a stone fireplace at one end of the bar. There are many large stuffed fish in glass cases around the top of the bar and on the wall. There is a conservatory garden room where children are welcome and a pretty garden which has two bird aviaries. A full menu is available as well as bar snacks and daily specials are also served lunchtimes and evenings, except Sunday evening. Dogs are welcome provided they are kept on leads.*

*1.00 a.m. - 2.30 p.m. Monday to Saturday*
*6.00 p.m. - 11.00 p.m. Monday to Saturday*
*Normal Sunday opening*

**Beers:** Fullers - ESB, London Pride
    Wadsworth - 6X

## Terrain

Mainly flat and easy going. At least two thirds of the walk is along the bank of a reservoir or canal and therefore is ideal for anyone interested in waterfowl or boats. One should reserve time to further explore the canal at Marsworth.

## Getting to the Start (Grid Ref.919140)

The walk starts almost opposite The Anglers Retreat at the British Waterways Car Park for Tring Reservoir which is also a nature reserve. Marsworth is on the B489 just north of Tring. There is a small charge for the use of the car park which at the time of writing is currently 50p per day.

## The Walk

**(1)** To start, continue through the car park with the banks of the reservoir on your right. At the end of the car park, follow the path ahead to soon find yourself walking between the Grand Union Canal on your left and the reservoir on your right. A few paces on where the path leads up the side of the bank on your right, take it and shortly after this turn right onto another path which runs between two reservoirs. Follow the path to the other side of the reservoirs to come out at a road.

½ mile **(2)** Cross the road and turn right to walk along the pavement the other side with another smaller reservoir on your left. When the reservoir ends, pass through a gap in the fence to follow a path along the edge of the reservoir on top of a raised bank (the dam). With the help of some steps cross over a concrete overflow to shortly after leave the bank of the reservoir by following the path ahead through undergrowth. Soon after, ignore a marked footpath on your right and continue to follow the main path ahead, to later pass a hide on your left used to spy on the birdlife on the reservoir. Eventually you will come out at a stile beside a gate, with the footpath continuing on your left.

1 mile **(3)** Go over the stile where you will see Sudbury Pumping Station on your left and follow a track ahead to a lane at Little Tring. Notice the old letterbox in the wall on your left. Turn left along the lane going uphill past some pretty cottages and follow the lane over what was once the Wendover arm of the Grand Union Canal. Immediately after this turn right onto a signposted public footpath, going over a stile and down steps into a field. The path runs along the righthand edge of the field with an indentation on your right marking the old route of the canal. On meeting a post approximately ⅔ of the way across the field, bear left to follow a grass track to the far left field corner. Go over a stile and immediately after, turn right over a second stile to thereafter proceed uphill along the righthand edge of a field. As you climb you will gain good views right of Ivinghoe Beacon, a distinctive hill at the end of a chain of hills which also acts as the end of the Ridgeway long distance path. The view is perhaps only spoilt by the cement works at Pitstone. On reaching the top of the ridge. You will gain another good view, this time ahead of you, over Wilstone Reservoir. At the far side of the field go over a stile and maintain your direction along the edge of the next

field. At the far side go over another stile and follow the footpath across the old course of the canal to reach a signposted crossing path, once the canal tow path.

**(4)** Go over the crossing path and a stile the other side and follow a path 1¾ mile downhill to soon come out at a "T" junction in the form of a track. Turn right along the track and follow it until you meet a field ahead, then turn left onto another track to soon meet and follow the bank of Wilstone Reservoir. An interesting thing about Wilstone Reservoir is you can still see the old hedgerows criss-crossing the centre of the water, marking the pattern of the fields before they were flooded. There are good views from the bank on your left to the magnificent wooded Coombe Hill and on your right to the church tower at Marsworth. Just before you reach the far side of the reservoir look out for a stile below on your right and at this point, walk or slide down the bank and go over the stile into a field. Continue ahead along the edge or the field and after a few paces go over a stile on your left to follow a signposted footpath the other side. Shortly after go over another stile and follow a path through a farmyard, usually inhabited by a rabble of noisy ducks and chickens. Just before you reach the far side of the farmyard go through a gate on

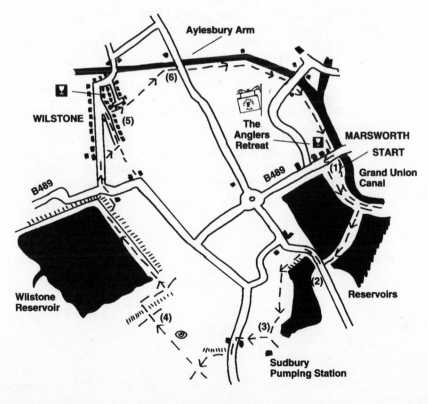

your right and immediately after, turn left to come out at the B489. Cross the road and follow the road the other side heading for the village of Wilstone. Just before entering the village pass through a kissing gate on your right and bear diagonally left across a field in the direction of a footpath sign. Pass through a gate on the lefthand side and follow a road ahead to soon come out at the village centre, identifiable by its small war memorial.

2½ miles **(5)** Our way from here is right along a signposted footpath to Dixon's Gap, however, if you are in need of an early drink continue ahead for a few more metres and you will arrive at the village pub, The Half Moon. Take the footpath mentioned which is a tarmacced path between houses and when this bends left, follow a hedged path ahead. Go over a stile and maintain your direction along the righthand edge of a field and at the far side, continue to follow the field edge round to soon meet a stile on your right. Go over the stile and follow the path ahead across the centre of the field, at the far side of which we meet the Aylesbury arm of the Grand Union Canal. *The original plan was to extend the Aylesbury arm to Abingdon where it would link with the Oxford Canal. Unfortunately the money to fund this project dried up and the Aylesbury arm was never extended beyond Aylesbury.*

2¾ miles **(6)** Turn right along the tow path to almost immediately pass under a bridge, thereafter continuing along the tow path heading for the tower of Marsworth Church directly ahead. The next stretch is delightful as you pass no less than four locks before the next bridge. Apart from the canal to keep you interested, there are fine views right across to Coombe Hill. Pass under the second bridge and continue to follow the tow path to shortly arrive at the junction with the main course of the Grand Union Canal and the Aylesbury arm. Leave the canal at the next bridge to come out beside The White Lion, a pleasant canalside pub though often packed with people trying to have a drink whilst having the best view of the canal. Turn right and pass the front of the pub to soon arrive at our recommended pub, The Angler's Retreat. After the pub it is a small matter of crossing the road to arrive at our starting point, the
3½ miles       car park at Tring Reservoir

# The Fox
# - Pirton

*Freehouse. The Fox is as pretty as the village of Pirton itself and is situated on the quiet High Street near the village church. With its red brick facade and pretty front garden the pub has an inviting appearance. The inside is tradltionally furnished with a fireplace at each end of the lounge. There is also a room to the rear of the bar where there is a pool table. A bar menu of light meals, sandwiches and snacks is available at lunchtimes and traditional fish and chips prepared by the landlady herself are served on a Friday night. Evening meals are mainly served on Friday and Saturday nights only. Occasionally live music in the form of a six piece band is performed on Saturday evenings. Children are well catered for, having thelr own children's room where games are provided and also a large play area outside. Dogs are also welcome.*

All day every day
Normal Sunday opening

**Beers:**  Flowers IPA
3 Guest Beers, one of which is always a strong ale

### Terraln

An undulating route over the chalk hills that mark the very northern tip of the Chilterns. Nearly all the walk is along tracks or through fields with constant fine open views. At the time of writing some of the fields have been left fallow and the enveloping natural flora can at times make the going a little hard though noticeably more attractive.

### Getting to the Start (Grid Ref, 146317)
The walk actually starts from The Fox which is at the centre of Pirton village. The village lies just west of Hitchin and is best approached via the B655 from where Pirton is signposted. Street parking is possible in the village.

### The Walk

**(1)** From the pub take the road opposite, Crab Tree Lane, and follow this round to the right of the village church, ignoring any turnings off, to later pass between two more pubs, The Cat and Fiddle and The Motte and Bailey, after which the lane bends right.

¼ mile **(2)** A few metres on when the lane bends sharp left and becomes Hitchin Road, cross the road to follow a signposted public bridleway ahead, passing to the left Pirton Court. The bridleway follows the course of England's oldest road, the Icknield Way, now a long distance path and runs in a straight line between high hedgerows. After an initial period of fairly easy walking along flat terrain, the Icknield Way gradually begins to climb the low hills which mark the very northern tip of the Chilterns. As you climb look out for a small mound in a field on your right. This is in fact an ancient burial mound known as a long barrow.

1¼ miles **(3)** After a steady ascent the track forks near the top and here you should take the lefthand track to follow a hedge on your left. First I recommend you follow the righthand track ahead for a few metres to enjoy

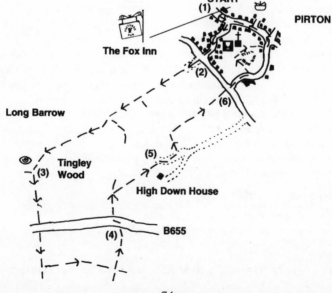

74

magnificent views over the Bedfordshire countryside and to the Barton Hills. If you have brought a picnic, this is a wonderful place to stop. Returning to the lefthand fork, as mentioned, follow the track which can at certain times of the year be a little undefined, therefore ensure you keep the hedgerow on your left. Later cross a road and join a track the other side signposted as a bridleway to Great Offley as well as to New Wellbury Farm. Follow the track for approxlmately 100 metres until you see a signposted footpath (yellow arrow) on your left. Take this and follow it across the centre of a field and at the far side pass through a gap in the hedge, maintaining your direction along the lefthand perimeter of the next field. After a short distance when the perimeter of the field bends sharp left, bear diagonally right across the centre of the field. On meeting up with the field perimeter again near the other side, with a path joining from the right coming from Old Wellbury Farm (whose rooftops are visible), turn left to follow the edge of the field with the hedgerow on your right.

**(4)** On arriving at the field corner, pass through a gap in the hedge ahead, cross a road and turn left to follow it for approximately 20 metres before passing through a gap in a hedge on your right to join a signposted public footpath. Follow the path in and out of a valley along the lefthand edge of a field and at the top, the other side, go over a stile at the field corner into another field. The path from here is diagonally right across the field, passing to the left of the magnificent Elizabethan High Down House, the chimneys of which are just visible, to reach a stile at the far corner. This field is often full of thistles and if you find this hard going, it is probably easier to follow a path ahead along the lefthand edge of the field and at the far side turn right, to follow the field perimeter down to the stile at the field corner.

2 miles

**(5)** Go over the stile and turn right along a track and after a few paces, left, to follow the lefthand edge of a field, the village of Pirton now clearly visible to your right. At the far side of the field (this is not always clear, but it is where a line of electricity wires cross the track overhead), leave the track to turn right, thereby continuing your route round the edge of the field wlth a hedgerow on your left and the electriclty wires following overhead.

2½ miles

**(6)** At the far side of the field, follow the road ahead into Pirton village and on drawing level with brick farm buildings on your right, take a signposted footpath on your left across a field heading for the church. As you cross the field you will see a series of banks and ditches. some of which are flooded. These are the remains of a Norman Motte and Bailey, the flooded ditch once having been the moat to the castle. Just before you reach the far side of the field turn right onto a crossing path and exit by a kissing gate at the corner of the field. Thereafter turn left along a lane and after a few paces turn left along the High Street, past the pretty village pond to soon after arrive back at The Fox, our starting point.

3¼ miles

3½ miles

# The Hampden Arms
# - Great Hampden

*Freehouse. This small pub has a comfortable, homely atmosphere, looking from the outside more like a private residence than a pub. It is in part over 400 years old and its first licensee was the Duke of Buckingham, John Hampden. The Hampden Arms is big on food, having 100 dishes to choose from! These are featured on boards throughout the pub, even in the entrance hall so everywhere you look there is a menu. As it is fairly small it is advisable to book should you wish to eat here. Its menu is not only large but also interesting, featuring items such as the Hampden Hedgehog and Hampden Nudger. Its cosy interior has two main seating areas, one being a room at the front of the pub, the other in front of the bar and a small seating area where the bar is situated. There is an interesting display of foreign currency at the side of the bar and the fireplace and beams accentuate the cosiness of the pub. It has a large garden with almost 30 tables should it be warm enough to sit outside.*

 *12.00 noon- 2.30p.m., 7.00p.m.- 11.00p.m.*
*Normal Sunday opening*

**Beers:**  Eldridge Pope - Thomas Hardy Ale
Greene Klng - Abbots Ale
Morland - Old Speckled Hen
Tetleys - Bitter
Wadsworth - 6X

## Terrain

Mainly flat along well marked woodland paths. For a time the route follows the course of the ancient earthwork Grim's Ditch though the undoubted highlight of the walk is Hampden House.

## Getting to the Start (Grid Ref.845015)

The walk starts from the pub at the village of Great Hampden. Apart from the pub car park street parking is possible beside the village cricket green. Great Hampden is easily accessed from three main routes. The A401 either side of Princes Risborough, the A413 between Wendover and Great Missenden and the A4128 between Great Missenden and High Wycombe. The village is well signposted from each road.

## The Walk

(1) To start, facing the pub, take the road to the right of the pub signposted to Bryants Bottom and High Wycombe. After a few paces turn right beside a bus stop and follow a signposted public footpath along the edge of the cricket pilch. At the far side of the cricket pitch go over a stile ahead to follow a path marked by white arrows through the wooded Hampden Common. Keep to the path, ignoring any turnings off to later, shortly after passing a large hollow on your right, arrive at a road at the far side of the common. Turn right along the road to soon arrive at a crossroads and here, take a public bridleway the other side of the road on your left, signposted to Speen. The bridleway bears left to run through the beautiful Monkton Wood. Once again ignore any turnings off, keeping to the main path and following the white arrows. What could be a very muddy path is vastly improved hy the fact that the route for horses (running parallel on the left) is separated by a fence from the path for, walkers.

(2) After approximately ½ a mile the path arrives at the far side of the wood where, after passing through some wooden rails, you will meet a crossing path marked by white arrows on a tree. Turn right onto the crossing path and follow this along the edge of the wood with fields on your left. The path continues along the edge of the wood for approximately ¾ of a mile, at one point passing a lovely flint and brick farmhouse, before eventually reaching a signposted public bridleway on your right beside a recently restored flint and brick cottage on your left. ¾ mile

(3) Turn right onto the bridleway (If you find yourself in front of the cottage you know you have missed the turning), and after a few paces keep left, ignoring a signposted footpath on your right. The way is now back through the centre of Monkton Wood and on your left through the trees you will glimpse a ditch and bank running parrallel with the bridleway. This is an ancient earthwork (probably Celtic) known as Grim's Ditch, which our route follows for the next 2 miles. As before, keep to the main path, ignorlng any turnings off, to eventually come out at a road running through the centre of the wood. Cross the road and join a lane the other side signposted to Redland End and Whiteleaf. Follow the lane (note the ditch and bank still running parallel on your 1½ miles

left), later passing a number of pretty houses on your left before arriving at a "T" junction. Turn left at the 'T' junction in the direction of the sign for Whiteleaf, and after a few paces cross the road and join a signposted public footpath on your right, also marked as a circular walk. After going over a stile, the path actually runs along the top of Grim's Ditch for a short distance before descending and once more running parallel with it. Shortly after descending from the ditch you should ignore a marked path (white arrow) off to your right, to continue along the more prominent path, marked at this point by a yellow arrow and still as a circular walk, and of course running parallel with Grim's Ditch on your left. As you approach the far side of the wood with fields in view ahead, ignore a track off to your left and continue straight on to shortly go over a stile into a field. Maintain your direction by walking along the lefthand edge of the field and at the far side ignore a track off to your left, to follow another track ahead in the direction of a white arrow, once more through woodland.

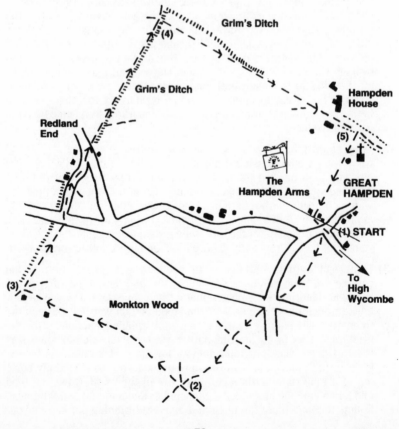

(4) After approximately 100 metres, just before reaching a stile ahead, turn right onto a crossing path marked by white arrows. Follow the path through a plantation which, in part, can be quite dense, to eventually arrive at the far side where the path bends left passing through some wooden rails onto a horse track. Cross this and pass through some wooden rails the other side and turn right along a path which runs parallel with Grim's Ditch (quite impressive at this point) on your left. Eventually the path twists right and passes through some more wooden rails to rejoin the horse track. Turn left at this point and follow the track, with a fence on your left, to soon arrive at a pair of gates at the corner of a field, with a footpath joining from the centre of the field on your right. Pass through the smaller gate and follow a fenced track ahead with the imposing Hampden House now in view, ahead to your left. The house though modernised in the 18th century to its current Gothic appearance, essentially dates from the 14th century. There has been a house on this site since the Norman invasion and it has always been the seat of the Hampden family, Earls and Dukes of Buckingham. The most famous of the Hampdens was John Hampden, the Parliamentarian and Cromwell's right hand man. John Hampden lived in the house up until 1643 when he was tragically killed in battle. On drawing level with the house, ignore a stile on your left but pass through a gate ahead, to thereafter follow the drive past the old stables on your right, after which you will arrive at Hampden Church.

2½ miles

(5) At the church turn right and take the tarmac path through the graveyard. The path leads round to the front entrance of the church where you should follow a grass path across the graveyard and pass through a gate the other side into a field. Continue ahead along the righthand edge of the field to shortly pass through another gate into a fenced area of scrub. It is worth stopping occasionally to look back at perhaps the best views of the church. Maintain your route ahead, passing to the right of a murky pond, after which pass through another gate to re-enter the field and maintain your route along the field's righthand edge. At the far side pass through a kissing gate beside an ancient burial mound and after a few paces cross a tarmac drive to follow a path ahead between fields. At the far side of the field, ignore a path to your left, continuing straight on, with the houses of Great Hampden now in view ahead. It is not long before you find yourself walking between the first of the houses and just after this, after passing through a gate, you will arrive at a narrow lane servicing the spread out dwellings of the village. Follow the lane ahead which bends gently left, bringing you to The Hampden Arms, our starting point.

3 miles

3½ miles

# 𝕿𝖍𝖊 𝕮𝖗𝖔𝖜𝖓 - 𝕻𝖎𝖘𝖍𝖎𝖑𝖑

*Freehouse. This has to be one of the most picturesque pub's in the Chilterns. Built of local flint, the pub is one of a collection of buildings including a 400 year old thatched barn encircling a well kept garden. The pubs facade and leaded windows is a picture at any time of the year but in spring when the ancient wisteria creeper is in full bloom, it could be straight out of a Grimm's fairytale. There has been an inn on the site since the 11th century, the current building dates from 15th century and boasts the largest priest hole in the country, large enough to hold 20 people. One monk, Brother Dominic, met a sticky end whilst hiding here. In attempting to save a young girl from the unwanted advances of a guest, he was run through with a sword. His ghost is said to appear regularly, wearing a black cloak and large hat. Ghosts aside, The Crown offers a warm welcome. Inside there are three interleading rooms in which to relax. All are carpeted and comfortably furnished with old photographs and plenty of copper and brass adding to the pub's charm. There is a blackboard menu available and a traditional Sunday lunch is served. The barn is hired out for functions and if you simply do not want to leave, the pub has a cottage available for letting, complete with a four-poster bed. No children are allowed except on Sundays and definitely no dogs!*

✗ ⼏ 🛏 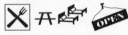 *11.30 a.m. - 2.30 p.m., 6.00 p.m. - 11.00 p.m. Normal Sunday opening*

**Beers:** Brakspear - Bitter

Flowers - Original

## Terrain

Mainly beautiful woodland paths passing in and out of typical Chiltern valleys. Some lovely views complement the walk, parts of which meet the route for The Stonor Arms

## Getting to the Start (Grid Ref.721878)

The walk starts from the BBONT car park at the Warburg Nature Reserve This is quite remote and care must be taken not to take the wrong turning. The easiest way to get there is to join the B480 from the A423 north of Henley and after passing through Middle Assenden, take a narrow lane left signposted to Bix Bottom. This is easy to miss so take care. Follow the lane for approximately 2 miles, ignoring all turnings off, to reach the car park which is on your right. The car park has a gate which is often shut but not locked.

## The Walk

(1) To start, leave the car park and turn left along the track by which we arrived and after approximately 35 paces go over a stile on your left to follow a narrow path uphill through the reserve. The path soon climbs the steep side of the valley and as you climb there are some good views behind over the reserve. As you near the top, ignore a path off to the left, keeping to the path you are on until it meets a track marked as the Oxfordshire Way,

(2) Turn left along the track and after a few paces bear right into a  ¼ mile
farmyard. Immediately upon entering the farmyard, turn left onto a track marked as a bridleway and still as the Oxfordshire Way. On entering a field ignore a path on your right and continue ahead along the lefthand field edge. As the field edge bears left, continue ahead across the centre of the field along a well defined path and at the far side, follow the path into a wood and maintain your route ahead along the lefthand edge of the wood. Cross a lane and join a path the other side, still following the Oxfordshire Way. The path leads through more typical Chiltern woodland and you should keep to the main path at all times, which is well marked by white arrows on trees, ignoring any turnings off. Later take a lefthand fork marked by a white arrow and the numbers PS17, keeping to the lefthand edge of the wood. Not long after, the path begins to descend the side of a steep valley

(3) At the bottom go over a crossing track and continue ahead, now along  1¼ miles
the righthand edge of a field. At the far side maintain your route ahead along a track ignoring a bridleway off to your left. After a short distance the track comes out at a tarmac lane, onto which you should bear right following the lane downhill past Pishill Church. There are some good views right at this point towards Stonor Park. Pishill Church despite its apperance was built in 1854. *In the last century a local man, Wiggins was prosecuted for relieving himself near the*

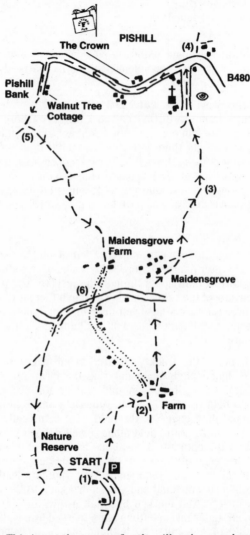

PISHILL

The Crown

(4)

B480

Pishill Bank

Walnut Tree Cottage

(5)

(3)

Maidensgrove Farm

Maidensgrove

(6)

Farm

(2)

Nature Reserve

START P

(1)

*churchyard. This is not the reason for the village's name however, which in fact means where peas grow.*

1¾ miles **(4)** At the bottom of the valley turn left to follow a road, taking care of the traffic as you go, to shortly arrive at The Crown Inn. After the pub, continue to follow the road (there are wide grass verges along which you can walk in safety) until it begins to bend left and at this point turn left onto a track signposted as a public footpath to Maidensgrove. The track leads back up the side of the valley to a cluster of houses known as Pishill Bank. As the track ends, follow a path ahead to pass to the right of Walnut Tree Cottage. After the cottage the path continues to climb the side of the valley through woodland and as it begins to level out, you should turn left onto another path marked with a white arrow and the number PS20.

**(5)** The path continues along the top of the valley (make sure you keep to the main path, ignoring all turnings off) and eventually joins a track shortly before arriving at the edge of a field. At the same time you will meet a crossing path marked by white arrows. Go over the crossing path into the field, still following the path marked as PS20. Continue along the righthand edge of the field where there are some lovely views left to the grounds of Stonor Park. At the far side of the field follow the path into more woodland, at the same time beginning to descend into another valley. Follow the path to the bottom and up the other side where at the top you will meet a stile which you should cross, thereby leaving the wood and following a fenced path between fields. At the far side of the field go over another stile and over a concrete drive, to join the gravel drive to Maidensgrove Farm. After a few paces turn right, passing through a white gate. then follow the gravel drive across Russell's Water Common.    2½ miles

**(6)** On meeting a lane turn right across the centre of the common. Continue until the lane begins to bend right, a distance of approximately 200 metres, and here leave it to join a track on your left signposted as a Public Right of Way, make sure you do not miss it. The track soon begins to descend into a valley, which is also the Warburg Nature Reserve. As it does so, ignore a marked footpath off to the right leading across a field. It is not long before you will see a sign for the Nature Reserve and after this the track descends through the woodland which covers the bottom of the valley. When you get to the very bottom of the valley, turn left onto a wide crossing track and follow thls back to the Nature Reserve Car Park, our starting point.    3¼ miles

3¾ miles

# The King Charles Head - Goring Heath

*Freehouse. The King Charles Head has a delightful setting surrounded by
500 acres of woodland, boasting its own two and a half acre garden. A copy
of the original pub sign hangs on the wall with a rhyme recalling a visit by
King Charles I. It is also said that the Great Train Robbery was planned at
this pub. The pleasant restaurant overlooks the large, lawned garden. The
traditional style bar is fully carpeted, so no muddy boots please, and has
two seating areas one at each end of the bar, both with bench seating and
stools. There is a brick fireplace with an interesting black stove and above
this is a cabinet display of golfing trophies. There is also a piano in the bar.
A serving dish lid display decorates one of the walls. A bar menu is
available serving a full range of snacks, main courses and delicious
desserts. Vegetarians are catered for.*

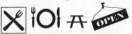 *10.30 a.m. - 3.00 p.m., 6.00 p.m. - 11.00 p.m.
Normal Sunday opening*

**Beers:** Brakspears - Bitter
       Boddingtons - Bitter
       Flowers- Original
       Marstons - Pedigree
       Wadsworth - 6X
       The above is a typical selection - changed regularly

## Terrain

After a steep climb out of the Thames valley the route follows some pretty woodland paths before arriving at the pub. The second half traverses a small valley before finally making a dramatic descent to Mapledurham. Apart from the intial climb the going is relatively easy.

## Getting to the Start (Grld Ref.670768)

The walk starts from Mapledurham village which is situated at the end of a dead end road. Mapledurham also has a country park, house and watermill, all open to the publlc and is well signposted from the A4074, just outside Caversham on the way to Wallingford. If you are doing this walk on a Bank Holiday or Summer weekend, it is better to park in the car park of the Mapledurham Country Park and combine the walk with a visit to the park, watermill and house. Alternatively, you can actually start at The King Charles Head where roadside parking is possible opposite the pub.

## The Walk

(1) From the village of Mapledurham, walk back up the road passing the entrance to Mapledurham Park on your left and continue later passing 'The White House', at the same time ignoring a signposted bridleway on the left. Follow the lane for approximately a further 200 metres until you meet the concrete drive to Bottom Farm on your left. Take the drive which is also signposted to Goring Heath 1½ miles, and later continue to pass through the farmyard and thereafter a couple of cottages on your right, immediately after which you should turn right to go over a stile into a field.

(2) Proceed gently uphill along the righthand edge of the field, climbing out $^{3}/_{4}$ mile of the valley and at the far side, go over another stile and maintain your route ahead, the cllmb now being a lot harder. As you climb it is worth pausing to look back at the view of Mapledurham House. On reaching the top and just before reaching.the far side of the field, go over a stile on your right and then turn left along a track. Stay on the track, passing Whittle's Farm, to later come out at a lane.

(3) Cross the lane and go over a stile the other side beside a gate slightly to $1½$ miles your right and continue ahead along the lefthand edge of a field. At the far side of the field go over a stile and follow a path ahead through woodland to eventually come out at a track at the woodland hamlet of Nuncy Green. Turn left along the track and after a few paces turn left onto a tarmac lane. Follow the lane past the houses of Nuney Green and just as the lane leaves the hamlet to re-enter the wood, turn right beside the drive to The Firs to follow a footpath through the wood marked by white arrows. Do not make the mistake of joining the track which forks right at the footpath. The footpath, which at times is a track in its own right, meanders through the wood, being well marked by white arrows and later arrives at a crossing path onto which you should turn left, still following the white arrows. Follow the path in and out of a valley and thereafter continue through the wood, still being guided by the white arrows, to eventually come out at a lane at the far side of the wood. Turn left along the lane to soon arrive at The King Charles Head.

**(4)** GOP over a stile opposite the pub and bear gently diagonally right across a small field. At the far side follow the path through a gap in the hedge and then after a few paces go right over a stile into another field. Turn left to follow the field edge and at the far side go over a stile and maintain your direction across the next field for approximately 30 metres, to then pass through a gap in the fence ahead and join a drive to a cottage on your left. Continue ahead along the drive and on meeting a narrow tarmac lane turn left. Follow the lane downhill until it becomes a track and turns sharp left in front of a beautiful half timbered, thatched cottage. At this point join a path on your right, signposted as a bridleway, passing to the right of the cottage and to the left of a farmhouse. Follow the footpath downhill through woodland, ignoring any turnings off, to eventually come out at the bottom of a wooded valley.

**(5)** Turn left along a track and after approximately 15 paces turn right onto a wide path, which leads up the other side of a valley. The path soon levels off and continues in a straight line through the wood You must keep to it, ignoring all turnings off, and later when the path forks keep left in the direction of a white arrow on a tree ahead. The way is now along a much narrower path which eventually leads to the far side of the wood, where you should go over a stile to come out onto open hillside. Here you are afforded a tremendous view over the river Thames.

**(6)** After admiring the view, proceed down the valley side to a stile visible at the bottom. Go over the stile onto a fenced path and turn left along the path and follow it until you eventually arrive at a lane. Turn right along the lane to retrace your steps back to Mapledurham village, our
starting point.

# The Red Lion
# - Bradenham

*Freehouse. The Red Lion is one of a collection of character buildings which make up the unspoilt village of Bradenham. The pub which is under the protection of the National Trust dates from the 18th century. The interior has recently been refurbished in late Victorian style. It has an unusual narrow bar between the public and lounge bars. The a la carte restaurant area leads off the lounge bar. The bar and bar rooms have wooden and tiled floors. The public bar has traditional dark furniture and the lounge bar and restaurant are furnished in attractive pine cottage style with pine panelled walls. An unusual feature of the lounge bar is the bright green tiled fireplace The rooms are uncluttered creating a feeling of space and light. A bar menu is available featuring snacks and daily specials and a roast is served at Sunday lunchtimes. No food is served on Sunday or Monday evenings. Dogs are not allowed and children are permitted in the restaurant and garden only.*

✗ ⚙ ♨     *11.00a.m.- 2.30p.m., 6.00p.m. - 11.00p.m.*
                              *Normal Sunday opening*

**Beers:**  Adnams - Ordinary Pale Ale  Brakspears - Old Pale Ale

**Terrain**
Mainly narrow woodland paths along valley sides. Apart from the attraction of the unspoilt Bradenham village, there are a number of spectacular views to be enjoyed along the way.

## Getting to the Start (Grid Ref.828950)

The walk starts from the car park at the top of West Wycombe Hill. To get there take the A40 to West Wycombe and opposite the entrance to West Wycombe Park, join Chorley Road, signposted to Bledlow and Bledlow Ridge. Immediately upon joining, turn onto West Wycombe Hill Road, in the direction of the signpost for West Wycombe Caves and the church of St. Lawrence. The lane runs behind the village before reaching the top of the hill and the car park.

## The Walk

**(1)** To start, from the car park, follow the lane by which you arrived, downhill, ignoring a marked bridleway left and approximately a third of the way down, turn left onto a signposted public footpath. This can be quite hidden in summer and can be easily missed, so keep your eyes peeled. Follow the footpath through woodland along the side of a valley before eventually twisting right (ignore a path to the left) to enter a field. Turn left along the edge of the field, thereby maintaining your route along the side of the valley, and at the field corner follow the path ahead into Hearnton Wood. Thereafter keep to the path through the wood, ignoring any turnings off, to after approximately ³/₄ of a mile, arrive at a 'T' junction with a more prominent path.

³/₄ mile   **(2)** Turn left onto the path going uphill and after a short distance, join and follow a track ahead to shortly after arrive at a crossing track. Turn right onto the crossing track and follow it along the top of a hill. Later the trees on your right give way to a new plantation where you have some lovely views over Bradenham village. Continue to soon after pass through a kissing gate and follow the track ahead, until you arrive at the newly restored Nobles Farm.

1¼ miles   **(3)** Turn right onto a narrow footpath (marked by a white arrow) opposite the farm entrance. Follow the path down the steep side of Averingdown heading for Bradenham. Near the bottom of the valley go over a stile, leaving the woodland to maintain your descent along the edge of a field. Go over another stile to proceed diagonally right across the centre of the next field and at the far side, cross a railway line with care and go over another stile and across a field, at the far side going through a kissing gate to meet the A4010. Cross the main road and turn right to arrive at The Red Lion.

1½ miles   **(4)** From The Red Lion follow the road into Bradenham village in the direction of the sign for the Youth Hostel and after a short distance, turn right onto a narrow lane which runs along the edge of the large village green. After approximately 30 metres turn left onto a track signposted as a bridleway, to continue skirting the green. The large house at the top of the green once belonged to Isaac D'Israeli, father of Benjamin D'Israell, one of our most revered Prime Ministers. At the far side of the green pass in front of the cricket pavilion and stay on the track which now passes to the right and follows the garden wall of Bradenham Manor. When the track forks at the corner of the wall, leave it to turn

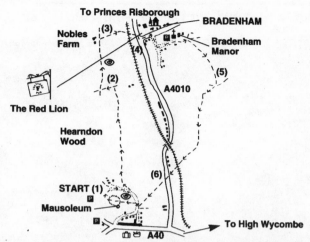

To Princes Risborough

Nobles Farm

(3)

(4)

BRADENHAM

Bradenham Manor

(5)

(2)

A4010

The Red Lion

Hearndon Wood

(6)

START (1)

Mausoleum

To High Wycombe

A40

right onto a signposted public footpath. The footpath which from here is marked by white arrows, runs through Pimlock's Wood and as on previous occasions, you should keep to the path ignoring any crossing paths or turnings off and taking heed of the white arrows.

**(5)** Eventually you will meet a marked path (white arrow) off to the left which you should ignore to maintain your route ahead along the valley side. Soon after this the church tower of St. Lawrence, crowned by its famous golden ball, will come into view ahead. Eventually the path bears gently right and starts to descend the side of the valley through some quite dense woodland. Shortly after, the path is bordered on the right by a beautiful line of beech trees. The path finally descends to the far side of the wood where, after passing through a gate, you will cross the railway line for a second time. At the other side after passing through a second gate, continue diagonally left across the centre of a field to soon meet the A4010, also for a second time. 2½ miles

**(6)** Cross the road and maintain your direction across the field the other side. At the far corner, leave the field and turn right along a lane. After a few paces take a path on your left and after going through some wooden rails, continue straight on up the side of Wycombe Hill heading for the mausoleum at the top. The mausoleum was built by Sir Francis Dashwood in 1765 to hold the hearts of members of the infamous Hell Fire Club which allegedly held meetings in the caves under the hill. (For a small fee these can be visited.) *The urns set in the walls were to hold the hearts but only one was put to use and that held the heart of Paul Whitehead. The heart was stolen in 1829 and Paul Whitehead is now said to haunt the hill and the valley below.* Pass to the right of the mausoleum to join and follow a concrete path through the churchyard of St. Lawrence. The path leads round to the church entrance beneath the tower. With your back to the door, turn right and follow a path out of the churchyard to the car park, our starting point. 3¼ miles

3¾ miles

89

# The Alford Arms
# - Frithsden

*There has been a pub on this site for at least 400 years though the original building which stood at the rear of the car park was burned down, probably in the last century, the present building dating from the beginning of this century. If you are a real ale lover you are in for a treat as the selection is not only the best for miles but the pub is unusual in that it is one of only a handful still left brewing its own beer. The Brew House can be seen next to the pub. Traditional pub food is served to compliment its own brews which is also sometimes a vital ingredient as in the beef and squirrel pie. Apart from the main menu daily specials including a vegetarian option are listed on a blackboard together with a changing selection of desserts. Everything about this pub right down to its Bar Billiards in the corner of the bar is traditional and it has a very 'local pub' atmosphere, obviously well used by local patrons who have been asked to name the pub's latest addition to its own beer range. The lower bar area to the rear is used for dining with the upper bar room being used for more serious drinking. Both areas are carpeted and traditionally furnished. An interesting display of beer bottles adorn the upper bar area. Together with a collection of foreign currency. A four pint Take Out Jug of Beer can be purchased which keeps beer fresh for up to four hours. There is seating outside on the patio garden at the front of the pub. Dogs are allowed in the garden or upper bar.*

     *11.00 a.m. - 11.00 p.m. All day every day*
                     *12.00 noon - 10.30p.m. Sunday*

**Beers:** Alford Arms - Olde Frithsden, Pickled Squirrel, Rudolph's
Revenge, a summer ale yet to be named,
Marstons - Pedigree
Morland - Old Speckled Hen
Wadsworth - 6X Whitbread,
Boddingtons - Bitter, Boddingtons Dark Mild, Castle Eden Ale,
Flowers - Original

## Terrain
Unnulating but fairly easy going following an equal combination of tracks
and field paths with a small amount of woodland walking. There are some
fine views to be gained, especially on the last stretch returning to Great
Gaddesden.

## Getting to the Start (Grid Ref.029113)
The walk actually starts from in front of another pub, The Cock and Bottle
at Great Gaddesden. The village is most easily reached via the A4146, north
of Hemel Hempstead, from where Great Gaddesden is signposted. As you
approach The Cock and Bottle, turn right (left if you are approaching from
Nettleden) into Church Meadow where street parking is possible. As
always, please be considerate to local residents.

## The Walk
(1) To start, facing Church Cottages, whlch are beside The Cock and Bottle,
turn rlght then immediately fork left, passing to the left of Great
Gaddesden School and follow the path ahead through the churchyard.
Follow the path to the church entrance and then bear left across the
graveyard to go over a stile at the corner into a field. Turn right along
the field edge and on meeting another stile on your right, go diagonally
left across the centre of the field, heading for the field corner ahead to
your left. At the field corner, pass through a gap in the hedge and
maintaln your direction across the next field, heading for the wood on
your right. Walk right up to the lefthand edge of the wood and go over
a stile, thereafter continuing straight on along the righthand edge of the
field, with the wood bordering your path on the right.

(2) On reaching the field corner go over a stile and turn left along a lane          ¼ mile
for a few paces and then immediately after passing the Amarabati
Buddhist Centre on your right, turn right onto a gravel drive, signposted
as a public footpath. After passing to the right of a cottage, leave the
drive and follow a narrow path ahead between fields. Later go over a
stile and maintain your direction along the lefthand edge of a field and
at the far corner leave a field and follow a narrow path ahead through
a small thicket into another field. Once again, maintain your direction
along the edge of a field, descending to the village of Nettleden, nestling
in the valley below.

(3) On arriving at Nettleden, turn left along a lane and after a few paces          ¾ mile
(unless you want to visit the church which is a little further ahead along
the lane) turn right onto another lane marked 'Unsuitable for Motor

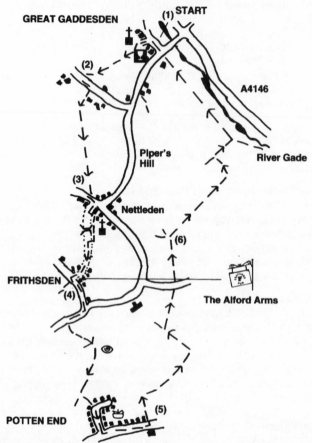

GREAT GADDESDEN

(1) START

A4146

(2)

Piper's Hill

River Gade

(3)

Nettleden

(6)

FRITHSDEN

The Alford Arms

(4)

(5)

POTTEN END

Vehicles'. The lane leads gently uphill, at first passing a row of
cottages, and when these end turns into a track. At this point look out
for some steps immediately after a drive on your left. Go up these to
follow a narrow path running parallel with the track, now on your right.
Later you will pass a bridge over the track where you will get a good
view of the flint and brick walls reinforcing the steep hanks either side.
The bridge was built to take a drive from the famous Ashridge House
(now a college) over the deep cutting. Continue to follow the path ahead
to later go over a stile, after which, turn right through a gate and then
left onto the track you were viewing earlier. Stay on the track, which
after a short distance begins to descend, ignoring all turnings off, to
eventually arrive at Frithsden, a collection of beautiful cottages. The
track naturally runs into the lane through the village and you should
follow this ahead (note a cottage on the right, 'Little Manor', with its
unusual tiled walls) at a fork keeping left to come out at the lane beside
The Alford Arms.

**(4)** To continue, as you arrive beside the pub, turn left along the lane and at a 'T' junction turn right in the direction of the sign for Potten End and Berkhamsted. After approximately 20 metres turn left onto a signposted bridleway beside Five Acre Farm. Follow this uphill between fields with the reward of good views left across to a large country house, Gaddesden Place. Stay on the bridleway, ignoring any turnings off, until you eventually arrive at a crossing path, immediately after passing a post on your left with a horseshoe and arrow pointing left carved into it. Turn left here and follow a narrow path uphill to come out at a cul-de-sac at the village of Potten End. Follow the road ahead and at a 'T' junction turn left and follow the road through the village, until you see a signposted public footpath to Great Gaddesden 1½ miles on your left. As a guide, this is just after passing Potten End Farm on your right. 1½ miles

**(5)** Join the footpath which at first runs alongside gardens of Potten End on your left, before descending through woodland, to eventually arrive at a stile to a field near the bottom. Go over the stile and immediately after turn right to follow a path to the field corner. Go over another stile and maintain your direction along the righthand edge of the next field with fine views over a sweeping valley on your left and directly ahead to Gaddesden Place. At the far side of the field turn left to follow the field edge round, heading for a farm at the valley bottom and approximately half way across, on meeting a wooden post with several yellow arrows, turn right and follow a well walked path downhill between fields, heading for another wooden post. At the post ignore a path on your right and continue ahead to go over a stile at the far side of the field onto a lane. 2¼ miles

**(6)** Cross the lane and go over a stile the other side and follow a path uphill through the centre of the field, heading for the wood above. At the top of the field go over a stile and follow a path ahead into the wood. At a fork, a few paces on, turn right and continue through the wood where at the far side (which is quite some distance) the path skirts left and where through a gap in the trees you gain a lovely view across the River Gade to Gaddesden Place. Shortly after this you will arrive at a 'T' junction with another path where you should turn right to follow the path downhill between fields. On meeting a field ahead go over a stile and then immediately left over a second stile, to thereafter proceed along the righthand edge of a field with the church at Great Gaddesden now in view ahead. At the far side of the field go over a stile ahead and follow a fenced path to shortly arrive back at Great Gaddesden, our starting point. 3 miles

4 miles

# The Bridgewater Arms - Little Gaddesden

*Freehouse. The facade of this 18th century building is more that of a country house than a pub. It was first licenced in 1815 and is an old coaching inn. In the mid 19th century a school was held in the pub for local children who had to climb through the window to enter and exit, as they were not allowed to go through the pub! A reminder of this period in its history is recorded in the title of one of the two restaurant areas being called The School Room. Children are still welcome here and younger children are catered for. The pub is large and spacious with a flagstone floor in the entrance hall and then carpeted throughout. There are two fireplaces in the bar area, one of which is transparent and the other having an array of pewter tankards hanging from its wooden mantle. Wooden beams, exposed brickwork, together with wooden and tapestry seats and stools give a cosy and comfortable atmosphere despite its spaciousness. There is a comprehensive menu consisting of snacks and light food, together with a full three course meal choice. A good wine list is offered and may be purchased by the glass or goblet, One or two interesting ephithets are chalked on the beams such as 'Best the ale drunk at the cost of others'! Who would argue with that! There is a small beer garden and dogs, although not allowed inside the pub, are welcome in the garden. It is requested that muddy boots be left outside.*

 *11.30 a.m. - 3.00 p.m., 5.30 p.m. - 11.00 p.m.*
*Normal Sunday opening*

**Beers:**   John Smiths - Bitter
Marstons - Pedigree
Websters - Yorkshire Bitter
Guest Beer from Tring Brewery

## Terrain
Fairly flat mainly following narrow or undefined paths through the extensive National Trust protected woodland and open common of the Ashridge Estate. Although not particularly tiring, careful attention is required to route finding and a good sense of direction is useful to complete the more difficult sections of the walk without mishap. This is the reason for the walk's C grade.

## Getting to the Start Grid Ref.971131)
The walk starts from the National Trust Bridgewater Monument at Aldbury Common. The car park is reached from the B4506 between Berkhampsted and the A4146 at Dagnall. The monument is signposted from the B4506. If for any reason the monument and car park are closed, then you can simply start the walk from The Bridgewater Arms. Parking is possible anywhere beside the lane on the way up to the monument.

*The Bridgewater Monument rises above the trees of the common to command fine views over the surrounding countryside. For a small fee you may climb to the top. The monument was built in 1832 to commemorate the third Duke of Bridgewater, then owner of the Ashridge Estate, and most remembered for his building of canals.*

## The Walk
**(1)** To start, from wherever you have parked on the lane to the monument continue to follow the lane until you have reached the monument itself. At the base of the monument, facing the entrance, turn right and go over a track to join a wide path the other side, marked with a blue arrow. Stay on the path ignoring any turnings off, to after a short distance cross a bridge. Continue to follow the path the other side, later passing to the right of a log cabin. Approximately ½ a mile after the log cabin the trees on your left thin out and there are good views of Duncombe Farm in the valley below.

**(2)** Not long after this you will see a path off to your right marked by a low wooden post with a blue arrow, a horseshoe and the number 4. Make sure you do not miss it. Take this, almost going back on yourself and follow the path through the wood to later come out at a junction of paths. Continue ahead here (ignoring all turnings off), in the direction of a post with an arrow and horseshoe, and then turn left onto a track, although you will still be continuing in the same direction. Take particular note of the last statement. Continue ahead, ignoring all further turnings off, to soon arrive at a fork with a post on your right

1 mile

95

and the number 5. Take the lefthand track at this point and continue to follow it through the wood, ignoring any further turnings off, including at one point a marked crossing path, to eventually come out at a gravel drive servicing a car park on your right. Follow the drive ahead to a lane and turn right along the lane to arrive at the B4506 at Ringshall.

1¾ miles **(3)** Turn right along the B4506 and after approximately 10 metres, turn left and pass through a kissing gate to the right of the entrance to Ringshall Pumping Station. After the kissing gate keep left and follow a narrow path through woodland with fencing on your left. After passing behind a red brick house go over a stile and follow the path ahead, ignoring any turnings off, to eventually join a lane which you should follow ahead. Stay on the lane until after approximately ⅓ of a mile you see two paths, one either side of the lane. These are not signposted so make sure you do not miss them. Take the path on your left and follow it to soon arrive at The Bridgewater Arms.

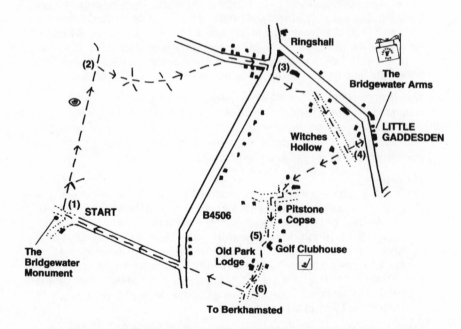

2¼ miles **(4)** To continue, from the pub retrace your steps back to the lane where we joined the footpath and cross the lane to join the path the other side. Follow the path downhill past the entrance to Witches Hollow and thereafter follow the path between gardens to shortly come out at the open woodland of Ashridge Park. Go over a crossing path and continue ahead uphill to shortly arrive at a golf green. Cross the green and go over a track the other side to follow a path ahead through woodland. After passing between gardens, turn left onto a tarmac drive and a few paces more at a 'T' junction turn right. Just after this, turn left along a tarmac lane, passing to the right of Pitstone Copse and follow the lane to soon arrive at the golf course car park and clubhouse.

(5) As you enter the car park, leave the tarmac to take a path on your right, 3¼ miles marked by a yellow arrow, passing to the right of rhododendron bushes. Shortly after this pass to the right of the golf club, then turn left to pass the front of it. Continue ahead across the fairway, passing a small green on your right used for putting practice. At the other side of the fairway, follow a track uphill through a copse, and thereafter after passing between some farm buildings, skirt to the left of a house ahead (do not turn left) Old Park Lodge, where the track becomes a tarmac drive which you should follow ahead.

(6) After a short distance the drive crosses a wide grass avenue bordered 3¾ miles by trees, where to your left you will glimpse the grand buildings of Ashridge College and to your right, the top of the Bridgewater Monument. Turn right here and follow the avenue heading for the monument and later cross the B4506 to follow a lane the other side, back to where you parked your car. 4 miles

# The Malster's Arms
# - Rotherfield Greys

*Brakspears. This traditional style 17th century pub has always been an inn serving the local community well, today being the focal point for Greys' Cricket Club. It is carpeted throughout with a dusky pink and dark wood decor. Original beams are visible and seating is upholstered and comfortable. The forces' connection of the landlord is shown in the pictures hanging in the restaurant and bar. A display of bugle horns can be seen on a beam above the bar and horse brasses add decoration to the restaurant, together with a brick fireplace on which a pair of bellows are displayed. Outside there is a patio and a large lawned garden which has recently been unfenced to provide an excellent open aspect with views across fields to the rear. Barbecues are held on Saturday nights and Sunday lunchtimes and on Friday nights when live music, such as Jazz evenings, takes place. The restaurant is table d'hote and there is a varied bar menu offering snacks, main courses, and a blackboard offering delicious desserts. Children are welcome and there is a children's room available. Muddyboots to be removed please before entering*

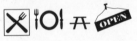

*11.30 a.m. - 2.30 p m Monday to Friday*
*11.00 a.m. - 2.30 p.m. Saturday*
*5.30 p.m. - 11.00 p.m. Monday to Friday*
*6.30 p.m. - 11.00 p.m. Saturday*
*Normal Sunday opening*

**Beers:** Brakspears - Old, Special, Bitter

## Terrain

This walk can be divided into two parts, the majority through fields and open country and about a third through woodland Generally the going is fairly easy though care must be taken to follow the right path through the woodland section of the walk. If walking between the months of April and September inclusive, it is worth leaving time to visit Greys Court which is passed en route

## Getting to the Start (Grid Ref.726824)

The walk starts at Rotherfield Greys opposite the village church. Unless you are using the pub, roadside parking is possible in front of the church. The village is best reached from the road passing the National Trust Greys Court between Henley and the B481. In between Greys Court and Greys Green take the lane signposted to Greys Church. This refers to the church at Rotherfield Greys which from the junction, is only ½ mile.

*The 13th century church is famous for a brass memorial to Lord Robert de Grey, a founder Knight of the Garter and the Knollys Chapel which contains a colourful ornately carved memorial to the Knollys family. An unusual story tells of a former vicar of the last century who to raise money for church funds, cultivated the white poppy in a nearby field for opium. Although the venture was a failure, the reverend won a silver medal from the Society of Arts and Sciences for his efforts.*

**(1)** To start, take the signposted footpath opposite the church (not the one to Henley) by passing through a kissing gate into a field, then continue straight on across the centre of the field. At the far side go over a stile and follow a narrow path downhill through a copse and at the far side of the copse, go over a stile into a field and turn right along the field edge. At the field corner go over a stile and continue along the righthand edge of the next field. As you near the far side of the field, ignore a stile on your right and continue to the corner to cross a stile ahead into a third field, immediately after which you should turn left and follow footpath 39 along the lefthand field edge. In summer this field is usually left to seed and is a beautiful carpet of Ox-Eye daisies.

¾ mile

**(2)** On reaching the top lefthand corner of the field, go over a stile and turn right along a track which in turn runs along the righthand edge of another field. It is not long before the track joins a concrete drive to New Farm (on your right) which you should follow ahead to arrive at a road. Turn right along the road and after approximately 20 metres, left onto a signposted footpath, going over a stile into a field. Proceed ahead along the lefthand edge of the field and at the far side, go over a stile to the right of a gate and maintain your direction along the lefthand edge of a second field. Later skirt to the right of a small copse, keeping to the field edge and thereafter proceed to the lefthand field corner.

**(3)** Go over a stile and turn left onto a well walked path marked by yellow arrows, which leads uphill through Lambridge Wood. After approximately 40 metres the path forks (make sure you do not miss this) with the yellow arrow forking right. At this point leave the marked path and fork left instead. After a few paces keep left to follow a path which keeps to the edge of the wood with fields on your left. The path combines with many other paths along the way but providing you keep to the edge of the wood with the fields visible on your left, you will not go wrong. Keeping to the edge of the wood, quite some time later, you will notice that once again the path is marked with yellow arrows. From here let the arrows guide you, at first keeping to the edge of wood with the fields still visible on the left, before taking a route across the centre of the wood to eventually come out at a lane beside a house on your left.

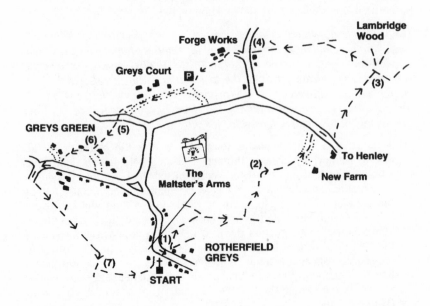

**(4)** Turn left along the lane and after a few paces, right onto a tarmac drive signposted to Forge Works. As the drive bends right, turn left and left again onto a signposted footpath. Follow this passing to the left of the Forge Works and thereafter go over a stile on your left into a field. Turn right along the field edge to shortly pass to the right of a murky pool. Thereafter continue along the field edge and at the far side go over a stile, maintaining your direction along the righthand edge of the next field. At the far side of the field go over a stile and maintain your direction ahead along the edge of a grassed area which acts as the National Trust car park for Greys Court. Note as you continue the brick maze on your right. Turn right along a tarmac drive, passing the National Trust oriental style ticket office and continue past Greys Court. If you have time it is worth stopping for an hour or so to visit the house. Although most of your attention will be on the house on your right it is also worth pausing to admire the view of the valley on your left. Unless visiting the house ignore the turnings off on the right and follow the drive past the house and downhill the other side. As it bends left near the bottom to reach a gate and a lane, leave it to follow a path ahead making for a stile.

**(5)** Go over the stile. across the lane and at the other side another stile. 3 miles and thereafter follow a well walked path across the centre of a field, making for a stile visible the other side. Go over the stile and follow the path uphill through woodland to soon come out at an area of open ground with an old barn. Maintain your direction passing to the left of the barn to come out at the cricket pitch at Greys Green

**(6)** Turn right and walk around the edge of the cricket pitch passing in front of the pavilion, and on meeting a road at the far side turn right to follow it, taking care of the traffic which at times can be quite fast. A short time on ignore a turning right signposted to Shepherds Green and continue for approximately 50 metres more to join a signposted bridleway on your left. After passing through a kissing gate follow a fenced path with a miniature golf course on your right and later pass through a gate and over a crossing track to continue ahead, still with the golf course on your right. Continue to follow the path, sometimes between thick hedgerows, until after approximately ½ a mile you see a stile on your left. This can be quite hidden in summer so make sure you do not miss it

**(7)** Go over the stile and follow a path gently diagonally left across a field 3¾ miles and at the far side go over another stile and maintain your route across the centre of the next field, heading for the church at Rotherfield Greys.  At the far side go over a stile and follow a path alongside the churchyard wall to come out between The Maltster's Arms and the church, our 4 miles starting point.

# The Shepherd's Crook - Crowell

*Charles Wells. This delightful 400 year old pub overlooking a small green with the village's Norman Church as a backdrop, is an essential part of a typically English scene, In the days when the pub was known as the Catherine Wheel it is alleged that John Runyan stayed here. The pub has recently been tastefully refurbished to enhance rather than destroy the attributes of the old building. On entering through its pine latch door it is a pleasure to find the pub is as pretty inside as out, having flagstone floors with rugs, exposed brickwork walls and wooden beams throughout. A wooden beam balustrade separates the bar area from the restaurant. An assortment of interesting country style furniture with pretty ruched curtains at the windows and several potted plants help to complete a relaxed setting. In the bar is a large brick fireplace with a high wooden mantle decorated with brass warming pans and oil lamps. Set into the fireplace on one side is the original oven. In keeping with the pub's name and so as not to forget its ver,y first customers, a shepherd's crook hangs on the restaurant wall. Glass cases of stuffed badgers and birds, together with old photographs of the pub and other rural scenes such as tilling and sheep shearing enhance the rural atmosphere. Outside there are seats on the patio and on the village green opposite. The restaurant offers a full a la carte menu served in the evenings from Tuesday to Saturday. A bar menu is available 7 days a week, consisting of sandwiches, snacks. main courses and desserts. A Sunday lunchtime roast is served but no food is served on Sunday or Monday nights. A children s menu is available.*

 *11.00 a.m. - 3.00 p.m., 6.00 p.m. - 11.00 p.m.*
*Normal Sunday opening*

**Beers:** Charles Wells - Bombadier, Eagle IPA
Guest Beers occasionally in winter

## Terrain
Very flat. Much of the walk is along tracks including a long stretch of The Ridgeway. Nearly all of the rest follows field paths. There are no ascents and the going is easy throughout.

## Getting to the Start (Grid Ref.726990)
The walk starts from the church at Aston Rowant. Aston Rowant is off the B4009 just north of junction 6 on the M40. The turning is signposted from the B4009 as Aston Rowant only. Follow the road round passing to the right of the church, after which you will find street parking possible.

## The Walk
**(1)** From the church walk back along the road by which we entered the village to the B4009, Cross the B4009 and join a track the other side, signposted as a bridleway. Follow this past Woodway Farm and afterwards a line of cottages and continue until you arrive at a wide crossing track, the ancient Icknield Way and the modern day Ridgeway long distance path

**(2)** Turn left along the track which follows the line of the wooded Chiltern escarpment on your right. This is no coincidence as when the track was first formed, it literally followed the bottom of the escarpment to take advantage of the springs which rise at frequent intervals at the base of the hills. Stay on the Ridgeway to much later go over a lane and continue to follow it the other side until you eventually arrive at a crossing track, signposted as a public Right of Way. $^{3}/_{4}$ mile

**(3)** Turn left here. heading away from the Chiltern escarpment and towards Crowell village and its pub The Shepherds Crook. The track continues between fields and when the large hedge on your right ends, you will gain good views right to one of the Chilterns' most famous landmarks, the Cement Works at Chinor! Eventually the track naturally runs into a single lane through Crowell village and you should follow this to soon arrive at The Shepherds Crook, behind which is the village church. 2 miles

**(4)** To continue, take the path to the left of the pub into the churchyard and walk through this to soon meet the B4009. Cross the road taking care of the traffic, to join a track the other side signposted as a deadend. Follow the track, at first passing some houses on your right and thereafter between fields, until you eventually arrive at a 'T' junction in the form of another ancient track, the Lower Icknield Way. 2½ miles

**(5)** Turn left along the track and after a short distance where the field ends, turn left to follow the righthand edge of the field. headng back towards the Chiltern hills. Approximately half way across the field the path bends right through a hole in the hedge and left to come out at

Kingston Blount village cricket pitch. Continue ahead along the lefthand edge of the cricket pitch and exit the other side via the car park. Thereafter follow a road between modern houses to a "T" junction. Turn left and follow the road for approximately 20 metres before turning right onto a signposted footpath. Follow this between gardens to arrive at a 'T' junction in the form of another path. Turn right here and after a few paces on your left you will see a gate in the fence. Pass through this to arrive at The Shoulder of Mutton pub. If for any reason it is locked, continue along the footpath to arrive at a road Brook Street. Turn left along the road, at one point going over a tiny stream, to arrive at a 'T' junction. To continue our route, cross the road and join a footpath signposted to Aston Rowant. However if you want to visit The Shoulder of Mutton pub lurn left along the road for a short distance and then left again up a driveway to reach the pub. If the gate is open, pass through it to arrive at The Shoulder Of Mutton pub. From the pub, follow the drive down to a road and turn right along to arrive at Brook Street on your right. At this point, turn left onto a signposted footpath to Aston Rowant.

3½ miles    **(6)** Follow the path along the righthand edge of a field and then alongside a cricket pitch, after which the path becomes fenced, to eventually arrive at a lane beside the village school. Follow the lane ahead to a 'T' junction in front of the village green with a cul-de-sac. Plowden Park, on your left. Cross the road and follow a footpath the other side which runs along the edge of the green. On meeting a road the other side, turn left and follow this through the village to arrive back at the village

4¼ miles    church, our starting point.

# The Lions - Bledlow

*Freehouse. Set in the picturesque village of Bledlow this pub was formerly called The Red Lion but its name was changed about 20 years ago. The building, 400 ,years old, is Grade I listed and was converted from three shepherd's cottages. The three open fires from these cottages are still used today and the plentiful dark wooden beams and exposed brick and stone walls lit only by subdued lighting and the flickering flames from the fires, create a cosy warmth lost to so many of our so called traditional pubs. The pub has a true country hostelry ambience helped not only by the loose rugs on the floor, log tables and traditional benches and pew seating, but by the genuinely warm welcome of the bar staff. As you enter, on the wall to the right, there are several old postcards and photos of the pub and details of its varied history. Hitler's aide, Herr Von Ribbentrop was once a visitor here. To the rear of the pub is a delightful cottage garden. The pub has a restaurant and a family room. An excellent bar menu is available serving hearty snacks and full meals together with a specials board. Dogs are welcome but it is appreciated if muddy boots could be left outside.*

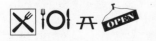

*11.00 a.m.- .00p.m.,*
*6.00 p.m. - 11.00 p.m.*
*Normal Sunday opening*

**Beers:**   Gales - HSB
John Smith - Bitter
Ruddles - Best Bitter
Wadsworth - 6X
Guest Beer - changed monthly

## Terrain

Nearly all through fields and over open grass hillside with regular fine views. Only one real ascent but as this is near the end of the walk it can be quite tiring. The path over Lodge Hill is particularly beautiful

## Getting To the Start (Grid Ref.777022)

The walk starts from the church at Bledlow where roadside parking is possible, but if you wish to have a drink or something to eat at The Lions before you start, it is worth parking at the pub itself which is a little further along the lane to the west of the church. To get to Bledlow, Church take the B4009. In between Princes Risborough and Chinnor and on reaching Bledlow turn into Perry Lane, signposted to Bledlow Ridge and Wycombe. Follow the lane under a railway bridge and shortly after turn right into Church End. The church is a little way along on the right and The Lions a little further still.

## The Walk

**(1)** To start, facing the church, turn right and walk along the lane through the village. A few paces on you will see a gate in a brick wall, signposted as the Lyde Garden. This is a pretty water garden based around the Lyde Spring and is open to the public. After the Lyde Garden, follow the lane to its end at a 'T' junction and turn left in the direction of the sign for Princes Risborough. After approximately 50 metres, turn right onto a track signposted as a public footpath. Follow the track past several houses and after the last house go through a small gate into a yard. Cross the yard and at the far righthand corner go over a stile to continue ahead along the righthand edge of a field. At the far side go over a stile and maintain your route along the righthand edge of the next field. Directly ahead you will see the chalk cut Whiteleaf Cross. At the far side of the field go over another stile and turn left along a path through a strip of hawthorn and after approximately 20 metres, turn right to enter another field.

½ mile   **(2)** Continue ahead along the lefthand edge of the field as though heading for the Whiteleaf Cross and thereafter continue in the same fashion (heading for the Cross) through a succession of fields, at one point crossing a pretty stream, to eventually go over a stile onto a lane beside the entrance to Manor Farm at Horsenden. Follow the lane ahead passing to the left of the village church to shortly after cross a pretty brook and continue past some idyllic cottages until you reach the entrance to Horsenden Manor on your right. This is opposite Gate Cottage. Go over a stile to the left of the entrance to the Manor and proceed along the righthand edge of a field with the grounds of the Manor on your right. At the far corner of the field go over a stile and continue in the same direction along the righthand edge of the next field. At the far side go over another stile into a third field beside a pond on your right. Again, maintain your direction through the field and at the far side pass through a kissing gate and continue along the lefthand edge of a garden. passing to the left of a house, after which you should follow the drive to come out at a lane at Saunderton.

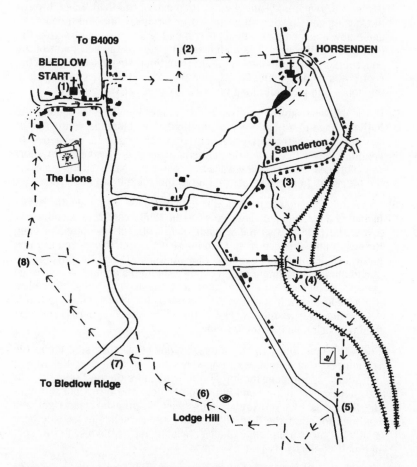

**(3)** Cross the lane and join a signposted footpath the other side to shortly enter and follow the righthand edge of a field. At the far side of the field pass through a large kissing gate, go up some steps and cross a single track railway line. Continue down the other side and pass through a second kissing gate to thereafter follow the righthand edge of a field. As the field perimeter gives way on your right continue ahead across the centre of the field, making for a house directly ahead. Pass to the left of the house and at the far side of the field. pass through a gap in the hedge to arrive at a lane in front of the 'Old Rectory'.

1¾ miles

2¾ miles **(4)** Cross the lane and head up the drive of the Old Rectory, skirting the tennis court and as the drive bends left to service the house, continue ahead to go over a stile at the corner of the garden into a field. Continue ahead bearing very gently left across the centre of the field and at the centre keeping to the left of a line of small trees, once the old field perimeter. As these trees bear right, continue to follow them and descend to reach a kissing gate at the edge of the field. Pass through the kissing gate to soon after cross over a railway line and then a stile and follow a fenced path which, after bending left, continues across the centre of a golf course. The path leads to a stile at the perimeter of the golf course. Cross this and thereafter continue straight on across the centre of a field, heading for a house the other side. Skirt to the left of the house and turn left along the drive to soon arrive at a lane.

3 miles **(5)** Cross the lane and at the other side follow the Ridgeway along the lefthand edge of a field. Keep to the field edge, climbing gently and at the field's top lefthand corner, pass through a gap in the hedge to continue your climb along the lefthand edge of the next field. A short way after go over a crossing track and follow the path and the signs for the Ridgeway (marked by acorns) up to the summit of Lodge Hill

3½ miles **(6)** From the summit of the hill you gain the best views on the walk, including a magnificent view across to the Whiteleaf Cross. Continue to follow the path across the summit of the hill, at one point passing through a line of beech trees to, after some distance, descend through natural chalkland scrub the other side. At the bottom of the hill proceed ahead along the lefthand edge of a field and after a short distance, go over a stile on your left into another field. Go straight across the centre of the field, two thirds of the way across going over a crossing track. After going over a stile proceed in the same direction across the next field to reach a lane at the far side.

4 miles **(7)** Cross the lane and join the Ridgeway path the other side along the lefthand edge of a field, with fine views to your right over the Vale of Aylesbury. As you near the top of the field ignore the first stile on your left, but go over the second into another field and turn right to follow the field edge. As you are walking ignore a stile on your right and continue to follow the field edge round. As you near the far side bear gently left away from the field edge. heading for a stile just to the right of a pair of electricity poles.

5 miles **(8)** Go over the stile and turn left along a track and after a few paces leave the Ridgeway, turning right onto a track signposted as a bridleway. Follow the track gently downhill, ignoring any turnings off, to finally arrive at The Lions of Bledow pub. Facing the pub, turn left and follow
5½ miles the lane through the village back to the church, our starting point.

## Ordnance Survey Landranger Map 175

# The White Hart
# - Shiplake Row

*Brakspear. The White Hart dates back 400 years and is an old ale house. Originally the building was thatched and at one point in its history was used as a butcher's shop. It has a delightful, pretty, well maintained garden, wilh wooden bench tables and seats, which is lawned with colourful flower beds, trees and shrubs. One side of the garden has an open aspect overlooking fields. Inside there is a comfortable bar and a restaurant area with wooden beams which extend into a conservatory. The bar has a large wooden fireplace blackened through years of use. The bar and restaurant are carpeted and together wlth traditional style wall lights and comfortable furniture, add to the congenial atmosphere. There is an extensive bar menu on a blackboard above the bar which is served from Monday to Saturday lunchtimes and Monday to Friday evenings. Sunday lunchtimes roasts only are served but there is a fine selection to choose from and a fish choice too. From Tuesdays to Saturday evenings an imaginative a la carte menu is available in the restaurant. A well-known TV chef sometimes brings his custom here which must say something for the quality of the food!*

  *12.00 noon- 3.00p.m., 6.00p.m. -11.00p.m.*
*7.00 p.m. -10.30 p.m. Sunday*

**Beers:**  Brakspears - OBJ, Bitter
Murphys - Stout

## Terrain
Although long this is an easy going walk with only one or two gentle climbs.
The first half of the walk is along lanes, through fields and woodland with
the second half following the Thames tow path back to Mill Lane. The
dramatic finale is the wooden walkway taking you to the centre of the river
and Marsh Lock.

## Getting to the Start (Grid Ref.771817)
The walk starts from the public car park at Mill Lane on the southern
outskirts of Henley. Mill Lane is reached via the A4155 on the way to Lower
Shiplake. It is signposted from the A4155 as the turning for Mill Lane
Sports Centre. Follow the lane over the railway line and the car park is
Immediately after on your left.

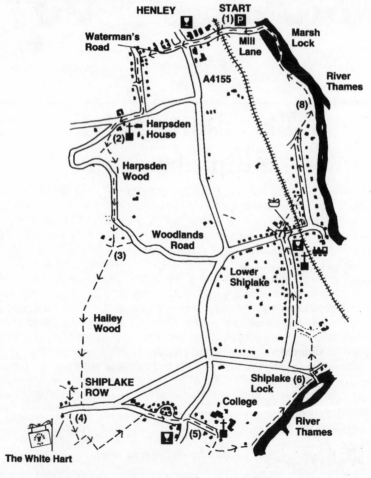

**The Walk**

**(1)** To start. turn right out of the car park and follow Mill Lane over the railway line to the main road, the A4155. Cross the road and take the road opposite. Waterman's Road, and after a short distance when this bends right, continue ahead along a signposted bridleway. After a short climb uphill this comes out at a road, Harpsden Way, onto which you should tnrn left. Follow the road, ignoring all turnings off, to eventually arrive at the entrance to Harpsden Court and to the right of this, the village church. Look out for a barn on your right at this point. The carved tiles which form the walls were originally used for printing patterns on wallpaper.

**(2)** After the church. follow the road for a few metres more, then turn left onto Woodlands Road and almost immediately after, left again onto a signposted footpath. This takes you uphill through Harpsden Wood, managed by lhe Woodland Trust. Near the top, fork left (marked by white arrows) and follow the path through the wood to eventually come out at Woodlands Road once more. Turn left along the road and follow it until it bends left beside a drive on your right to Redhouse Lodge. At this point, leave the road and follow a signposted footpath ahead which, after running between houses, soon arrives at a narrow tarmac lane.  ¾ mile

**(3)** Cross the lane to enter a field the other side. opposite Little Spinneys, and bear diagonally right across the centre of the field, heading for a spot roughly 20 metres left of the far right hand corner. At the far side go over a stile and follow a track in the direction of a yellow footpalh arrow through the centre of Hailey Wood. Ignore all turnings off to come out at the far side of the wood and thereafter follow a track ahead, going over a crossing track as you do so, to walk between fields, with good views to your left across the Thames valley to Berkshire, Later you will meet a more prominent track on a bend and here you should turn right along the track, to shortly meet a wooden bungalow on your right. At this point leave the track by passing through a gap in the hedge on your left and thereafter continue along the righthand edge of a field. At the far side pass through an old gateway to meet and cross a road and arrive at The White Hart  1½ miles

**(4)** To continue, facing the pub, pass through a gap in the fence at the lefthand perimeter of the car park, into a field. Once in the field turn right, and then bear diagonally left across the centre, heading for the far corner, identifiable by a pair of electricity poles. On reaching the far corner turn left, almost going back on yourself, to follow a path between fields. After a short distance turn right to then follow the lefthand edge of the field on your right. Follow the field edge almost two thirds of the way across until you meet a stile and footpath on your left. Go over the stile and thereafter follow a track ahead to eventually (after passing through a kissing gate) join a drive to a farm on your right. Follow the drive ahead to a road and turn right along the road until you meet the A4155 beside The Plowden Arms.  2½ miles

3¼ miles **(5)** Cross the A4155 and follow Church Lane the other side to its end at the church at Shiplake. *The church which dates from the 12th century is ramous for having staged the wedding of the poet Alfred Lord Tennyson to Emily Sellwood.* Keep to the right of the church passing through a gate with a sign, Shiplake College Private, and immediately after this bear right to join a narrow footpath which runs steeply downhill. As a guide, this is directly opposite the church entrance. On meeting a junction of paths at the bottom with a field on your right, turn left along a track and follow this to. after passing some boathouses, come out at the River Thames. Turn left and follow the river along the tow path until you reach Shiplake Lock.

4 miles **(6)** On drawing level with the lock go over a stile in front of a brick wall and turn left to shortly meet a road. Turn right and after a few paces opposite Mill House turn left over a stile and follow a fenced path between fields. Go over another stile and continue ahead along the lefthand edge of the next field and at the far side, go over a stile on your left into another field. Bear diagonally right across the corner of the field to meet a drive the other side. Turn left along the drive and go over Lash Brook to meet a lane. Turn right along the lane past the first houses of Lower Shiplake and continue, ignoring all turnings off, to eventually arrive at a crossroads beside The Baskerville Arms your last chance for a drink before the finish.

4¾ miles **(7)** Turn right at the crossroads, along Station Road, and immediately after crossing the railway line, turn left onto an unmarked path. After a short distance turn right onto a crossing path, to pass through a kissing gate and follow another fenced path. Go over a gravel drive and just after this turn left along a residential road, passing between a number of magnificent houses. Ignore all turnings off and keep to the road which bends right after the entrance to Bolney Court and eventually ends in front of a private drive. Here take a fenced path on the left which runs parallel to the drive, passing a magnificent garden complete with its own miniature railway. Go over a stile then a wooden plank bridge into a field to shortly meet the River Thames once more.

5½ miles **(8)** Turn left to follow the river and when the field eventually ends pass through a wooden gate to start the undoubted finale of the walk. This is a dramatic excursion into the middle of the river along a wooden walk way which takes you to Marsh Lock. After the lock, continue along the walk way passing in front of the weir, where at weekends you often find brave canoeists practising their skills, to shortly arrive back on dry land at Mill Lane. Follow the lane ahead and you will soon arrive back 6 miles at the car park from where we started.